winning table tennis

winning table tennis

Tim Boggan

Henry Regnery Company·Chicago

Library of Congress Cataloging in Publication Data

Boggan, Tim.
 Winning table tennis.

 1.Table tennis. I. Title.
GV1005.B64   796.34'6   75-32967
ISBN 0-8092-8155-4
ISBN 0-8092-8151-1 pbk.

Copyright © 1976 by Tim Boggan
All rights reserved.
Published by Henry Regnery Company
180 North Michigan Avenue, Chicago, Illinois 60601
Manufactured in the United States of America
Library of Congress Catalog Card Number: 75-32967
International Standard Book Number: 0-8092-8155-4 (cloth)
                                     0-8092-8151-1 (paper)

Published simultaneously in Canada by
Beaverbooks
953 Dillingham Road
Pickering, Ontario L1W 1Z7
Canada

acknowledgments

I would like to thank Mr. Hikosuke Tamasu, editor of the Japanese *Table Tennis Report:* in the last five years I have learned much about table tennis from the pages of his fine magazine, and I owe him a debt for several anecdotes and ideas that I've used in this book.

I would also like to thank the USTTA, its officers and members, for allowing me the opportunity to write about table tennis over the last ten years: my avocation as reporter-editor of the USTTA magazine *Table Tennis* helped make this book possible.

The cover picture and pictures of me at the New York Table Tennis Club were taken by Nick Sorrentino. All other photos have been individually acknowledged in the text.

contents

Tim Boggan playing a Friendship Match before 4,000 in Shanghai, April, 1971. (Photo by George Buben)

preface

When I was in Peking on our famous "Ping-Pong diplomacy" trip in the spring of 1971, our lowly United States team (we were not then ranked among the top 20 teams in the world) was being magnificently feted by the Chinese, who, a week earlier in Japan, had dominated the World Table Tennis Championships. Of course the eyes of the world were on us, and everyone at our "friendship first, competition second" dinner parties sought repeatedly to present as united a front as possible around one after another of the circular tables that always contained, along with the hot and the cold, the sweet and the sour, both Chinese and Americans.

Naturally our hosts were very intent on not embarrassing us during our stay in China, especially during our table tennis play before 18,000 spectators in Peking's Capitol Stadium. The Chinese could have skunked us 11 matches to 0, but very considerately just edged us out 6 matches to 5. Moreover, their players, coaches, managers, photographers, and reporters were often intently telling us over and over again that they were learning a great deal from us. *What* they were learning from us, especially about table tennis, I could never figure out. But that didn't stop me, the very well treated guest, from unconsciously feeling the need to continue the deception.

One afternoon, while I was practicing with a Chinese player who was being very nice—"feeding" me high balls and of course nearly effortlessly returning almost all my drives—I grew bold and seriously began smashing the ball in, using my peculiar "no look" forehand. I have this deceptive habit of smacking the table tennis ball as if I'm hitting a golf ball and not lifting my head until the ball is well on its way to wherever it's going—which in golf doesn't prevent me from bringing up my head in time to watch the flight of the ball, but which in table tennis often doesn't allow me time to follow the shot until I've already hit in a winner or seen that the ball is going to come back to me.

Anyway, when my Chinese opponent complimented me on hitting in his setups and mimed my peculiar swing with nodding approval, I couldn't swallow my pride, took the bait, and in the spirit, really, of reciprocating the man's good fellowship, began immediately to demonstrate more clearly to him how I hit what might be the most individual table tennis shot in all the United States or, what the hell, even the world.

Wow! No sooner did I take this interest, hook myself into this subject, than he quickly called over to the side of the table two interpreters, who in turn quickly called for two flashbulb photographers, who in turn quickly called for a reporter who began jotting down some things in his red notebook.

Yes indeed, this Chinese player wanted to make it plain to all the world that *he* was learning something from *me,* his new-found American friend.

Understandably, the image has long lodged itself in my mind—I guess because, at the deepest level, I really wanted to feel that I *could* be of value to this fellow human being who, instructions aside, really, I thought, wanted to learn, to be nice, to be decent to me. So, O.K., I agreed to be his foil, China's foil (if that's what I was), because I wanted to complement him who was complimenting me. I sincerely wanted to believe and bear objective witness to the fact or (it didn't make any difference) the illusion that, as the Chinese kept saying, "Everybody can indeed learn something from everybody else."

Now, four years later, you, my obviously real pupil, are about to open this book proper (or improper). I hope of course that what I've learned thus far in my table tennis life and am sharing with you here might be the truth and might help you. More, though, I hope the book is what you—like that faraway (but still so table-close) Peking man—might be willing to give the compliment not of a lie but a few hours' or at least somewhere a few minutes' illusion to. The illusion, the belief, that, yes, I can teach; that, yes, you can learn . . . something.

chapter one

your introduction to
my table tennis life

My earliest recollection of playing not table tennis but Ping-Pong was with my father in the basement of our house in Dayton, Ohio, in the sandpaper and hard rubber bat days of the late 1930s and early '40s. I loved the lights over the table and the indefinable darkness around it, the green and white colors that seemed so clear and beautiful to me, the sound of the racket in the silence steadily hitting the ball.

One night my father beat me in a game, which—though he might by then have been giving me less than 15 points—was very unusual. To make matters worse, it was the last game of the evening and I had no chance to get back at him. As he moved heavily up the cellar steps, I stood there at the bottom and cried and carried on terribly. When my dad got to the top of the stairs, he turned slowly around and said, "You didn't want me to *let* you win, did you?"

1

And I, looking up, sobbed, "No!"

Naturally you realize, or at least suspect, that my father, quite contrary to what he'd said, had indeed let me win almost all the games we'd ever played together. Only this particular night for some reason he hadn't. And because he hadn't, I'd learned even more about winning—how it wasn't any good if you didn't do it all by yourself. I guess it was something I'd always known but deep-down had to be reminded of—a truth thereafter that, try as hard as I could and though I sometimes failed, made all excuses pointless and all losses bearable until the next win.

Physical as table tennis obviously is (demanding of you very fast hand speed, very fast footwork), it is yet more mental (demanding of you the split-second ability to act decisively—with confidence and, above all, with enthusiasm). My father didn't know much about Ping-Pong, but being a four-letter man himself, he was clenched-fist enthusiastic about all sports. So when he saw I was serious about Ping-Pong, he didn't think there was anything sissy about it and so devoted all his considerable psychological energy into using that game (as well as, later, baseball or basketball or golf) to make me a winner.

No surprise then, that 30 years afterwards, with my father long dead but even longer very much alive in my memory, I was in another basement, far away from that first one, teaching my own sons not Ping-Pong but table tennis. (Scott is now 14, Eric 12—I started them playing the sport when they were 5.) And that, like my father before me, I was letting them win 95% of the time—though of course they didn't know it (and didn't want to know it either).

I've always agreed with those people who thought that, whatever your sphere of interest in this world, the losing will take care of itself but that it's important, particularly for beginners at anything, to learn and keep learning about winning. So my sons had to at least try to think like winners. And to that end, I never consciously finished a practice session with them that they didn't hit in the last, winning shot.

When we first started "practicing," if my 5-year-old, looking up almost from under the table, made any contact with the ball at all, I'd praise him. Instead of it being my point, it would become his. Gradually the game between us became more complicated. If the boy could just get the ball over the net, whether it hit my side of the table or not,

1974 U.S. Under-11
Champion Eric Boggan
(shown here in 1971 when
he was eight years old)
demonstrating his basic
backhand block.
(Photo by Bill Marlens)

Any coach's most important
clenched-fist word—"Fight!"
(Photo by Raul Rodriguez)

1974 U.S. Under-13 Finalist Scott
Boggan (shown here in 1971 when he
was ten years old) demonstrating
perfect balance as he drives home a
forehand winner. (Photo by
J. Rufford Harrison)

3

again it would not be my point but his. Then, achieving more control, he had to get the ball on my side of the table to win the point. In the next stage, I also had to miss it—which I would learn to do quite often.

And my boys have done well. Regardless of the fact that their games have developed differently, my boys have been winners. Scott, in 1972 when he was 10, won the U.S. Under-13 Doubles Championship and in 1974 was the runner-up in the U.S. Under-13 Singles Championship. Eric, at 10, was also the U.S. Under-13 Doubles Champion and in 1974 was the U.S. Under-11 Singles Champion.

Of course they've done so well not just because I, their coach and confidant, know something about winning, but because they've played seriously in tournaments and so necessarily have had to play against so many different kinds of players with so many different styles. No father can be a substitute for practical experience. And naturally it's the same with you who read this book. Unless you're committed to serious play against players better than you, my coaching, my psychic support, won't by itself allow you to be the very good player you obviously want to be in reading *Winning Table Tennis*.

Believe me, it's to my own advantage, my own credibility, that I speak to you straight. Surprisingly, despite my early instinctive yearning for the game, I never had the advantage when I was growing up of the kind of tournament practice I'm early in this book urging you to take. Sure, like hundreds of other kids, novices at the sport, I'd won a couple of casual youth organization cups. But I never had the "professional" junior play that my own kids have had—or in fact that any good player I can think of has had. I did not play anything but casual Ping-Pong until I was 19. And only when by chance I met a fellow at my university who was into the real table tennis scene did I know that such an underground United States Table Tennis Association tournament circuit even existed.

Right, before I go any further, I anticipate your questions. How can you find out about tournaments, where and when they're played? And where clubs to play at are in your area? How can you see pictures of and read about the superstars of the sport? Get addresses of foreign associations—in China, Sweden, Japan—and subscriptions to their pictorial magazines? Where can you learn all the changing rules of the sport and how to buy the latest and best equipment—rackets, balls, tables, even a practice robot? Very simple. You write to me for my table tennis magazine, the one I officially edit for the USTTA that goes all over the U.S. and to 120 foreign countries. Here's the address:

TABLE TENNIS
12 Lake Avenue
Merrick, New York 11566

You won't be out of the scene for long.

But back in your introduction here to me. I've always liked board games, table games. Ping-Pong, I feel, is the strategic extension of a sitting-down-to-think game. The emphasis on a player's positioning of self to best advantage, his need for perfect timing, his ability to finesse (to make controlled, deceptive placements) on his way to planning and completing a succession of shots, is instinctively challenging to me. It makes something like a universal appeal to my game-struck unconscious. This sport, so popular in the mystic East, combines all the fascinating mental play of a board game with the go of quick physical action. It therefore makes an almost religious appeal deep inside many a person—like the pleasing onomatopoetic word "Ping-Pong," like the balancing yin-yang (the sitting-moving, passive-active suggestion) of Chinese philosophy (the Chinese, of course, are the best table tennis players in the world)—in that it offers a way to bring peace and harmony to one's too often aggressive being.

But in the beginning, untaught, uncoached as I was, there were lots of things I didn't know.

I'd won a number of my early matches against what you'd call today Class B players by being steady. Had stayed at the table and relentlessly pushed and blocked ball after ball. Until one day an enormous turning point in my approach to the game occurred.

Being young and sort of a wise guy I began mimicking a player I was beating who had a very odd forehand. Surprisingly, by using this silly forehand I started to win points. Started to beat this player at his own game by continually taking over the offense and hitting the ball through him. What fun!

After that, I took to being an aggressive player and gradually formed my own highly individual "no-look" forehand. I became just as relentless an attacker as I had been a defender—became,

5

specifically, a serve-and-one, what you call third-ball hitter. Incredibly enough, if I hadn't tried to copy, however jokingly, that weak player's crazy forehand, I might never have become a good player. The moral of this story therefore must be, "Whatever your imagination seizes on must have some truth for you. Be individual enough, have sense enough to learn from it."

It's really strange how you make your own discoveries in this sport, this little sphere of action, how you add new strokes and shots to your repertoire. The first tournament I ever won was the Dayton City Championship and in the final I upset a nationally ranked player solely by improvising a sort of backhand lob or balloonlike half defensive-half offensive return that I was as much astonished by as my opponent, who had played me in practice and thought he knew my game thoroughly. It was a classic case of that old saying, "Necessity is the mother of invention."

The next tournament I was looking to win was the Ohio State Championship, and on my first real try I lost 22-20 in the deciding 5th game. At the time this was a terrible blow to me, for I had lost to a defender whom I'd allowed, by too carefully playing his push, push, push close-to-the-table game at the precarious end, to pick-hit two balls through me.

At any event, I wanted to be a winner and I had just lost by not being aggressive enough. So I vowed then and there never to let anyone else take the initiative against me, at least not if I could help it, not if the score was close. And in all the years that followed, I've held quite well to that little promise to self.

The next year I won the Ohio State Championship. Then, on going to graduate school at Indiana University, I won the Indiana State Championship. From 1950-56 I must have played in 100 tournaments. At the time I was living in the Midwest, I won the U.S. Intercollegiate Championships twice.

The sad fact, however, was that I, as a serious player, happened to be at a great disadvantage. I had to take my competition where I could find it. Not only did I start the sport at the very late age of 19 but by chance I was in a pocket of the country where, although there was considerable interest in the game, there was little competition for me on a very high level. Then, as now, almost all of the best players came from just a few sections of the country, mainly the New York City area. So however much I might practice, I could not get much better.

I did, however, become the 7th ranked player in the U.S. and in the mid-1950s was picked to be on the U.S. team in the U.S.A.-Canada International Matches at Toronto. Finally, after so many rides to and from tournaments, so many dark roads, so many repetitive matches, I reached what I thought was that last decisive point, the one so many competitors in whatever sport feel is the losing end—the point of diminishing returns. And yet I was only 26 years old.

So, O.K., I know what it is for young kids to play this game. And older kids too. In the next 10 years I was away from the sport, I learned some other things. But they will not come into a discussion of my life here.

Only once from 1956-65 did I enter a table tennis tournament. In 1960 my wife and I happened to be in Washington, D.C., while the U.S. Open was being held there. Impulsively I entered and lost in the second round—after which I didn't stay to see a single match..

In 1965—it was spring—I chanced to read in a local newspaper of a Long Island tournament. By this time I had a teaching job at Long Island University in Brooklyn, a wife and two children, a home in Merrick, and I felt pretty stable. I called for more information about the tournament and was invited to a private little club on the Island to practice. This again was a turning point in my table tennis life.

At the age of 35 I came back into the game—and started all over again. Returned, in fact, in fantasy, with perhaps more enthusiasm, more imagination, for the sport than I'd ever had previously. No, I had not changed—not, anyway, so far as my love for table tennis was concerned —but, as I was soon to find out, the sport was not quite the same.

Five days after I'd played that one night at a little club in Rockville Centre (and was beaten by everybody), I entered the state-like Long Island Championships—and lost in the second round. It turned out that my opponent, like practically everybody else in the tournament, was using what to me was a strange pips-in, flat-surfaced "sponge rubber" racket. It was different from my late 1940s-50s hard rubber pips-out bat in that it was multi-layered thicker and gave a different spin to the ball.

I lost to this player not only because of course after that long absence I hadn't any table control or forehand touch, but because I had

7

particular difficulty with what my opponent called his high "lob" return of my forehand drive. The ball kept bouncing and spinning to the side much too high for me to hit comfortably—and I just didn't know what to do with it.

It was clear if I again wanted to be one of the better players—and I certainly did—I would have to move with the times, get a sponge racket, and start practicing against the very best players I could find.

Which I did. Actually, making this adjustment was very easy for me because, aside from my new bat having a layer of sponge under the outside hard rubber pips, it wasn't much different from my old one.

Moreover, not only was I able to play exactly the same kind of block-and-hit, close-to-the-table style game I had played 10 years earlier, but my playing weight was soon the same—and, with practice and my renewed enthusiasm, my hand and foot speed were as fast as ever. Granted table tennis was ideally a young man's sport (if you weren't a World Champion by the time you were 23, the odds were definitely against you), I was still only as old as I felt—and teaching young people had kept me young.

This time, too, I had a great positional advantage in that I was living in the New York area. Now there was an even better basement where I (and, in time, my boys) could go to and play—at the bottom of a New York hotel. Down in this darkness my subterranean sport flowered. It was *the* table tennis club in the country—where almost all the best players in the country played. And where there was a great deal of card table action as well. What had I been missing all these years? What if I'd come here earlier? No telling how I would have played and what I would have been like.

Anyway, the next year, 1966, I was the Long Island Champion—just as years before I'd been the Ohio and then the Indiana Champion. That year, too, our New York team of Dick Miles, Jack Howard, Fred Berchin, and I won the U.S. Open Team Championships. In the late 1960s I began beating some of the best U.S. players (Dell Sweeris, who was then number three in the country, and Danny Pecora, the 1966 U.S. Open finalist and 2-time Canadian Open Champion). I even threw a scare into our undefeated U.S. Champion Dal-Joon Lee. In 1968 in the U.S. Open Team Championships, I skunked D-J 21-8 the first game of our match, and for a moment it

Winners and runners-up awaiting their awards in the 31st World Championships at the Aichi Stadium in Nagoya, Japan, 1971. Tim Boggan is second from left. (Photo courtesy of Zdenko Uzorinac)

Tim Boggan, runner-up in World Championship Jubilee Cup (for players over 40), receiving his beribboned medallion from Mr. Koji Goto, President of the Japanese Table Tennis Association in Nagoya, Japan, 1971. (Photo courtesy of Zdenko Uzorinac)

looked as though I might be the first player in this country to beat him—but, amazingly, he would not lose a single tournament for the next four years.

They say life begins at 40—and for some time now I was beginning to be absorbed with the idea of trying to organize and direct not just my own game in my own little area but the whole state of the sport in the U.S.

In 1969 I became a Vice-President of the USTTA.

In 1970 I took over the editorship of the table tennis magazine I'd been sometimes writing long articles for for four years. I immediately enlarged and expanded it fourfold, into a tabloid newspaper format, picked up more advertising as I went along, and, as our membership doubled, I began sending *Table Tennis* round the world.

In 1971 I went to Japan as a USTTA delegate to the International Table Tennis Federation's policy-making meetings. In the World Championships at Nagoya, in the Jubilee Cup (for players 40 or over),

9

Premier Chou En-lai of the People's Republic of China greeting Tim Boggan as a member of the historic "Ping-Pong diplomacy" group in Peking, April, 1971.

I defeated the 1954 World Men's Singles Champion Ferenc Sido of Hungary, which was my best win ever, and then went on to become the runner-up in this event—losing in the final to the Czech "Laci" Stipek, a former 3-time World Doubles Champion.

And then, carefully timed for the last day of this world tournament, the impossible happened. The U.S. table tennis team was given a surprise invitation to come immediately, through the bamboo curtain, into the People's Republic of China. Our 15-member group would soon be playing table tennis in Peking and Shanghai before thousands and thousands of spectators.

Friendship Matches between the Chinese and Americans before 18,000 in Peking's Capitol Stadium, April, 1971.

And this was just the beginning of the new world that had opened to me in this most international of all games. From now on, I knew, I would be traveling and playing abroad.

That summer I was playing with invited team members against the French in Paris.

In 1973, as President of the Association, I led our delegation to the World Championships in Sarajevo, Yugoslavia.

In 1974 I was playing in an Invitational in Jamaica and rooting our U.S. team of Danny Seemiller, George Brathwaite, and Angelita Rosal to victory over the English.

11

U.S. Team to 1975 Calcutta World Championships (standing, left to right): Angelita Rosal, Captain Tim Boggan, Judy Bochenski, Olga Soltesz, Peter Pradit; (kneeling) Dal Joon Lee, Lim Ming Chui, Danny Seemiller, Paul Raphel.

Just recently, in February of 1975, I captained the U.S. team to the World Championships in Calcutta.

My table tennis experiences in these interesting places, what I've learned about the sport from watching or even on occasion playing against some of the best players in the world, I'm naturally going to detail from time to time in the instructional parts of this book.

But before I begin trying to teach you how, in this great social leveler of a sport, you can assert yourself and rise up in the tournament ratings, I want to emphasize that if you diffuse your playing energies over the years as I've diffused mine, you just can't become the winning player you imaginatively hope to.

The sport is not only for the very young—I'm obviously proof of that. For, regardless of age, of commitment, I'm at 45 one of the 50 best players in the United States. In 1974 I won the U.S. Senior (Over-40) Championship (and also the two other biggest Senior tournaments of the year, the Eastern and Canadian Opens).

There is for me a great joy in winning. It's my mind, my imagina-

Norbert Van de Walle (right) on defeating Bobby Fields in the semifinals of the U.S. Open, New York, 1962. (Photo courtesy of Mal Russell)

tion, my will that sometimes brings dream to reality in this game that for 35 years now, come what may, has been a part of me.

Almost telepathically, almost mystically, I feel I direct that ball with my racket to a target—like an archer raising and letting fly the arrow from his skillfully felt bow. In fact, in fantasy, my hand position when I'm balanced and at the ready to quickly whip the ball in for a winner is very much like an archer with his bow brought up and bowstring back. I feel ready not only to loose this one shot but to take quickly arrow after arrow from my magic quiver and send them thud again and again into the all-embracing circle of self and targeted opponent opposite.

There is a supreme joy in the coordination, the conjunction, of mind and body working together to position, aim, shoot this most personal of spheres into the imaginative life-and-death center of a man. Winning table tennis over the years, says the child, says the father of the man, *is* fun.

chapter two

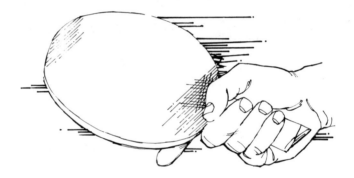

I know a tournament player (in "real life" he's a mechanical en-
gineer, into design and construction) who makes his own balsa wood
center racket, and (it's part of his fun) rubber bands a couple of dozen
popsicle sticks around the handle of his very thin blade. He says it
gives him "more control."

Of course, whether you quickly come to find such highly personal
adjustments bordering on the absurd or imagine for the longest time
that they will one day bring you more than modest success, the fact is
that you can't hope to be a winner without having your own personal
racket. And since I'm assuming you're reading this book because you
want to get good fast, if only at first to beat your friend on the next
block, and so sooner or later will play in tournaments to work at
quickly improving your game, I'm going to begin at the beginning and

the racket,
the grip, the ball

tell you what rackets are both legal and available to you, and then discuss some of the advantages and disadvantages of each.

As of 1975, according to the USTTA, your racket may be of any size, shape, or weight—but it may not have any white, yellow, or brightly reflecting edge-bindings around it. The blade itself must be of wood—and it cannot have a cork or ball-destroying sandpaper covering. The rubber on both sides of the racket must be of a uniform dark color. If, as with some penholder players, only one side of the racket is covered, the wooden side must be of a uniform color with the rubber side—but the wooden side must be stained, not painted, this color.

TYPES OF RACKET

Practically everyone I know plays with the standard-*size* racket you can pick up at any sporting goods store. But, as you are about to see, there's plenty of room for individual preference, particularly when you're talking about *quality* rackets, which you can buy only at the very best sporting goods stores or from the various dealers at a tournament. These sponge bats cost from $3 to $35 apiece, depending for the most part on the ''ball-gripping'' quality of the rubber that covers them and with which experts particularly know how to impart the many different kinds of spin that make up what the game is all about.

Tournament players use the following surfaces for their rackets: (1) plain wooden, (2) hard pimpled rubber, (3) sandwich (pips-out) sponge, (4) inverted (pips-in) sponge, (5) anti-topspin sponge, (6) a two-sided combination of any of the above.

Let me discuss each of these in detail, and at the same time try generally to prepare you for the specific Basic Strokes chapters that naturally follow this one.

Plain Wooden Surface

Back in the 1920s, when organized table tennis was just getting started in the U.S., the 1922-24 Kansas City Champion was using a racket cut from pressed wood. And abroad, in Hungary in 1925, where the best players in the world were beginning to develop the sport, everyone owned a wooden racket and played a very close-to-the-table half volley or blocking game.

Today, 50 years later, almost no one (except for an occasional ''freak'') uses wood (or, were it legal, sandpaper) on both sides of his racket, for the simple reason that other surfaces, particularly sponge rubber, are so much more effective in putting speed and spin on the ball. Penholders, however, who, in greatly favoring their forehand, use only *one* side of the bat and prefer a lighter racket, often have no covering, just the wood, on the *other* side of the bat—and using this wooden side sparingly, at strategic times, can effectively mix up their spin to win a much-needed point. (Naturally the way a spinning ball bounces off wood is not the way it spins off other surfaces.)

Hard Pimpled Rubber Surface

From the 1930s on into the '50s, this hard pimpled rubber surface was the kind almost every serious player was using. The wooden blade had been covered on both sides with a thin layer of pips- (or pimples-) out rubber. At the time this revolutionized the sport—in that the new catapulting surface allowed for attack-and-retrieve play much farther away from the table.

Many competitors, in the U.S. especially, were later, despite the advent of the next, sponge rubber, revolution, very reluctant, even into the '60s, to give up this hard rubber surface. It demanded correct, graceful, tennis-like strokes from the successful player and more often than not produced a clearly definable contest of overspin and (a neu-tralizing) underspin play between a hitter and a 20-feet-back-from-the-table chopper. Players also liked the light hard rubber racket for its maneuverability and because its thinly covered surface (legally, its thickness must not be more than 2 millimeters on each side) enabled them to "feel" the ball and so gave them greater control and, like many a writer preferring a pencil to a typewriter, greater aesthetic satisfaction.

Today very few tournament players still use this racket—and those who do use it, even on one side for spin variation in their play, are almost exclusively older players in their 30s, 40s, or 50s who grew up learning the game with this surface.

Sandwich (Pips-Out) Sponge Surface

In 1952, in India, a little-known Japanese player named Satoh astounded the table tennis world by introducing a new kind of "sponge rubber" racket with which he won the Bombay World Championships. Very soon this technological advance caused such controversy everywhere among players and officials that certain kinds of sponge bats were ban-ned, or not banned, until finally the International Table Tennis Federa-tion (ITTF) decided on some standards. (Now the total thickness cover-ing each side of the racket cannot be more than 4 millimeters.)

The sandwich (pips-out) sponge, which is the kind of bat I use (be-cause I'm a blocker and flat hitter and because it provides the best transition from the "old" game to the modern-day one) consists of (1) a single layer of sponge over the wooden blade and (2) a sheet of the old pips-out rubber over the sponge. This sponge, of course, is not like the household sponge but is the cellular type, so that, when the layer of rubber is glued tightly over it, the gas within is trapped and when struck gives off an elastic bounce to the ball that makes this racket surface considerably more "alive" than the old hard rubber racket one.

Most troublesome, too, to the old-time player is the cushioned silence this racket produces. Hearing the ball (there used to be a famous blind umpire who once worked the final of a U.S. Open without making a mistake) was so important to those who played in the 1930s-'50s that Raoul Bedoc, a former French World Team Captain, could quote one of his players as saying, "I have a cold today, and cannot hear well, which is why I cannot play well."

No wonder, then, that some great U.S. players, most notably Marty Reisman, could never psychically make the transition from hard rubber to soft, spinny sponge.

Today, for stylistic reasons, only a small minority of the best professionals in the world use this pips-out sponge racket—and they are almost all Chinese or Japanese penholders, are not "spinners" but fast, close-to-the-table quick hitters, blockers, and what in recent years we've come to call jabbers. Some few good shakehands players, though, use this type rubber on *one* side of their racket, almost always on their backhand, both for offense and defense.

Inverted (Pips-In) Sponge Surface

This is the racket used by the very best shakehands players in the world. The same cellular layer of sponge is placed over the wooden blade, but then the rubber sheet with the pips is turned *face down* onto the sponge. As a result, the possibilities for ferocious top and side spin greatly increase, whether the player winds up and loops the ball hard or takes a short, sometimes awful-looking jerky stroke that would so offend a purist a generation ago.

Anti-Topspin Sponge Surface

I first saw this strange black bat used by a bearded Frenchman named Jean-Paul Weber in the 1971 World Championships in Japan. It was

Penholder pips-out hitter Lim Ming Chui of the U.S. Team. Force of mind and body in perfect concentrated balance. (Photo by Mal Anderson)

whispered about that he had discovered it, like a strangely surfaced Cezanne painting, in some obscure hand-me-down shop in Paris. This anti-spin racket offers little or no resilience and so effectively absorbs the vicious topspin imparted by the inverted racket. As you might guess, it's most effectively used by the defensive player who's looking to confuse his attacking opponent by deadening, neutralizing, his topspin.

Two-Sided Combination Surface

There are a number of interesting individual possibilities here, depending of course on what kind of game you want to play. For example, if, like the number-one U.S. player Danny Seemiller, you use Austrian flat-surfaced anti-spin rubber on your backhand (to backspin, deaden the ball) and Fujii Ultra D rubber on the forehand (to enliven, give a hop to the ball), and both sides of your racket are the same seemingly undetectable shades of red, and you're fast enough to keep twirling the racket in your hand (ready to use either side) as your opponent serves and you're waiting to receive the ball, you can really give the fellow opposite you problems trying to figure out what kind of spin is on your return.

Or if, like penholder Lim Ming Chui, our number-two man at the Calcutta World Championships, who has only the one side of his racket covered (with pips-out rubber), you suddenly, unexpectedly, use the other, wooden side, you can really destroy your opponent's timing. (Oh, I remember one time I had Ming match point when he did this to me and I was caught completely off guard.) Even our very experienced 3-time U.S. Champion Bernie Bukiet was once reported to have said when Chui was repeatedly using the wood against him, ''I know I can't beat him. The wooden side of his paddle drives me crazy. I can't stand the thump, thump of the ball against the wood, and when the ball comes back to me it does nothing.''

WHICH RACKET SHOULD YOU USE?

I know, of course, if you're just starting to play seriously (and have all the desire in the world to succeed), how confusing it still is to try and pick the bat that will win for you. But just as my two boys and I all use different kinds of rackets, depending on our individual styles, so too must you experiment and decide for yourself which is most emotionally comfortable and effective for you. The more you watch and study the great players in action, the more you see that each is his own man.

What it all comes down to is this: Can you win with what you use? Half a dozen years ago, on the advice of my knowledgeable friend Dick Miles, I tried switching from pips-out to pips-in rubber for a tournament period of six months. During this time, I broke several inverted bats in anger after losing some close matches in which, try as I might, I just couldn't hit in forehands with my usual control. Finally I gave up the smooth-surface racket—it was just not for me.

However, I do think, to begin with, you should determinedly try either pips-out or pips-in sponge and, unless instinctively you're a chopper, stay away from the anti-spin.

Disadvantages of Wood, Hard Rubber, and Anti-Spin

Obviously, wood on both sides won't allow you to spin or hit the ball hard enough, won't allow your chop defense to "take" well enough —and once your experienced opponent catches on to the at first unusual effects of your racket, you won't have much chance of beating him.

The hard rubber surface, which is still played with here in this country by the Iranian star Houshang Bozorgzadeh and our 3-time U.S. Women's Champion Patty Martinez, enables the player to have a good touch, is excellent for in-close table control, and always, in this new age of sponge topspin, presents the hope of confusing the opponent who is not used to its "dead" block or half block-half chop possibilities. After all, it was ironically Miss Martinez herself who said, on losing in Calcutta recently to a girl from Hong Kong, a throwback hard-rubber player like herself, "Boy, that's a weird racket!"

But, let's face it, even if you're Marty Reisman, the most spectacular of hard-rubber-bat players, the guns against you today are just too all-whirling powerful—and once your spin from yesteryear becomes recognizable, you'll be shot down like with radar.

21

The new anti-topspin surface is very effective if you're de-fending—but, after experimenting with it initially, many players have had to give it up. Because of its deadening properties they haven't been able to hit well enough with it. More and more it's become a surface for one side of the racket only—to be coupled with an inverted sheet for attacking. That hasn't always worked out so well either, though, because if your anti-spin is, say, on your backhand side, it's a dead giveaway you aren't about to loop or flick or counterdrive with much force from that side (not unless you can find time in the middle of the action to twirl, change the side of, your racket).

Differences Between Pips-Out and Pips-In Sponge

Anyway, since it certainly seems you ought to start off using sponge rubber that will allow you to attack, perhaps if I discuss here the differ-ence between sandwich pips-out and inverted pips-in, you can better begin to make up your mind. Possibly, for steady backhand control against an attacker, you'll end up using pips-out on one side and, for opening the point with a loop of your own, pips-in on the other side.

Although most coaches would tell you to use the inverted bat —would even point to former penholder World Champion Hsi En-ting as an example of those great players who in recent years have switched from pips-out to pips-in, I can't say—I don't want to say—that you must start off with the smooth-surface racket. After all, the pips-out offers what a beginner needs, more control, and, besides, I'd like to at least imagine that some shakehands player (as well as penholder) could win the World Championship using the racket I myself use.

True, the last two shakehands World Champions, Stellan Bengtsson of Sweden and Istvan Jonyer of Hungary, have used Mark V or Sriver inverted rubber—but it's also true that the great pips-out Chinese players, universally acknowledged World Team Champions (whose "Friendship first, competition second" ideology strongly prohibits a clean-up of too many World Championship titles), have proved on the international circuit that they're quite capable, on the given day, of beating any European smooth-surface player, be he World Champion or no.

Mostly the difference between the two rackets comes down to

whether you want to "spin" the ball or quick-hit it. I want, like Chuang Tse-tung, the famous Champion of the '60s, to stay close to the table, to temporize if need be with fast blocks and pushes until (the sooner the better) I can snap-hit the ball in with a short, and therefore more controllable, in-close-to-the-body stroke. To that end I naturally want a racket that features the complement of control to my over-the-table stroke. Although I can play my style well with any size pips, the larger they are the better—for then there is less surface area for the ball to contact and less unpredictability in the way the ball is catapulted off the racket.

The looper, of course, uses the inverted racket with all its hard-to-control surface area that shoots the ball upwards, so his thick, heavy, pips-in sponge produces lots of top or side spin. He may bring his stroke slowly, deliberately up from his knees and just graze the top of the ball or, something like a discus thrower, start arm curled behind him and swing all out—but in either case the ball will arc up and so will not have the "kill" speed or the lower, line-drive trajectory of the flat-hit pips-out bat.

Naturally, as you read on, you'll see the strategic reasons why one wants to loop or not loop—so that inevitably your choice of racket will be dependent, even more than whether you play with the penholder or shakehands grip, on the style of attack or defense that best suits you.

If you play penholder and have a sponge-rubber covering on only one side of your racket, quite clearly, unless you make some other adjustment, the bat will be lighter than it would be if you played shakehands. Some say the heavier racket is best—as in baseball, the heavier the bat, the more power it's capable of. But also with such a racket (it may be a thick one-ply, as opposed to a slower multi-ply), the more difficult it is in high-speed table tennis not only to quickly swing through the ball but to control it. The very thickness and heaviness of the paddle makes it more difficult to maneuver in your hand. Perhaps that's why when the Chinese team made its reciprocal visit to the U.S. in 1972, we saw one of their players in practice swinging a pretend two-pound steel racket.

If you're going to use a light paddle, one thing seems certain: you'd better, like the up-close-to-the-table Chinese, be aggressive—which means, as you'll see shortly, that you'd better have marvelous foot-

23

work, because you're not going to do too well back from the table if a heavy looper swings his demolition ball at you.

No racket covering is perfect—I myself in very warm, humid weather have to suffer my own dripping sweat getting lodged down in between the pips on my racket and giving a glazed, slippery surface to it.

Just as good players on their way to becoming great players experiment with different kinds of racket surfaces (can you imagine any defensive player worth his salt who didn't try the new anti-topspin bat when it came out a few years ago?), so too do an imaginative few continue seeking further technological advances in the sport.

At the World Championships in India last spring, the Chinese created quite a stir when some of their new team members, who had never appeared previously in international competition, started making a few of the best men and women players in the world look like near beginners. This was possible only because these particular Chinese were using new Tientsin-made stickier-than-anything-ever-seen-before inverted surfaces.

But although some cried foul, it only reminded others of what one wit said when the sponge revolution wiped out the hard rubber enthusiasts 20 years ago, "The way our rackets are improving, all we have to do is put two paddles at the table and let them play."

How the Chinese Pick a Racket

While I'm on the subject of the Chinese, perhaps it would be interesting for you to know how these great players select their rackets. Take Li Ching-kuang, for instance, who is the best blocker and jabber I've ever seen. (That Stellan Bengtsson rallied to beat Li on his way to winning the 1971 World Championship was nothing short of miraculous.) In Calcutta, Li was explaining to Lim Ming Chui of our U.S. team how he'd finally picked out the racket he had in hand.

"First," he said, "you go through several boxes of paddles to find one that you like. Then you sand it—to remove the excess weight of the paint. Then you look at it to see if it has any wood cracks. At which point you make your first rejection. Then you knock on the bat all around. If it makes a hollow sound any place, you reject it." According to Li, Chui's bat made lots of hollow sounds. Except, said Ming, he didn't hear what Li Ching-kuang heard. "Then," said Li, "you take a ball and begin bouncing it on your racket. The ball should stay in one position. If it does, you've got a pretty good racket." The ball on Chui's racket hopped in all directions.

So if you think you've got a problem selecting your racket, think of our experts, think of the sport's superstars—then do the best you can with what you've got.

How Experts Take Care of Their Rackets

As you're coming now to realize the importance to a player of his own individual racket (compare weapon in hand to a larger-than-life gunfighter like "Shane"), you ought to know, to begin with, that you don't clean it by wiping the surface with racket-eroding sweat or saliva. Like the Chinese, you use water.

As for changing the often expensive rubber, replacing the sheets—well, that's up to you. Pips-out will last longer than pips-in. But you'll know after a while when your racket starts to go dead. Just before winning the Canadian Open a couple of years ago, Danny Seemiller was telling me how every two weeks or so he'd have to take the inverted sheet off his forehand and replace it because it didn't remain "hard" enough. "Slow" rubber, though it might be good for a beginner, wasn't any good for him because the ball that he wanted to fast loop stayed too long on his racket. As for the anti-spin on his backhand—it could be left on forever.

Usually it's easy for good players to get (the rectangularly cut) replacement sheets of rubber. (Conveniently, the rubber and its sponge backing come already glued together.) Sometimes players are in the business and would be very happy to sell you the sheets you need that you can't get at your sporting goods store. It's when you have to epoxy your 15-year-old cracked blade and/or handle back together again for one more precarious time that you have to worry.

When you do get your replacement sheets of sponge rubber, you can quickly learn, with a little knowledge and practice, how to put them on yourself. The way I started to learn was to have several drinks in a hotel bar one night after a tournament with our 6-time National Champion Dal Joon Lee. I began jotting down on a paper napkin as

Six-time U.S. Champion Dal Joon Lee: " . . . use fingernail polish or lighter fluid to clean all the old sponge off; and sand it down with sandpaper. . . . "

best I could what he was rapidly telling me, and —surprise—it later came out so clear and logical that I risk passing it on to you here.

"First," said D-J, "clean the blade of the racket thoroughly—use fingernail polish or lighter fluid to clean all the old sponge off; and sand it down with sandpaper. Second, make sure the surface is dry and then glue the outside of the blade first and move clockwise in toward the center. A half tube of glue is too much—use about a third. Third, fold back the rubber sheet with its sponge backing in half and rub clockwise on the racket, then open the sheet and continue rubbing. Fourth, slide the rubber sheet off the racket. Do not put any more glue on the rubber—you can put more glue on the edge of the blade. Fifth, allow the rubber and racket to sit for 5-10 minutes until any wet spot dries—that way there won't be any bubbles. Sixth, put the sponge-rubber sheet down, on the handle end first, and shove it in, then smooth it out flat and turn the racket over. Gently press. Seventh, cut to the shape of your blade on the side where you can see where you're going. Use a pair of sharp scissors, not a razor. Eighth, play.''

Sounds too much like work, does it? Well it surely won't after you get into winning. And, you'll see, you'll soon be very fussy, very careful with your racket.

In the years I've traveled with professional table tennis players around this country and abroad, I haven't yet seen one—not one of them—fail to carry his racket(s) *with him,* in an enclosed case, whenever he had to hop from big city to big city, most often by plane. And only once have I read where a famous player, Sweden's World Doubles Champion Kjell Johansson, unaccountably had his racket(s) in his baggage—and where, sure enough, there was a mix-up that sent the Swede's belongings not to Bucharest but Budapest. This was a mistake so strange that when Johansson, who of course hadn't his own personal racket and who'd refused to borrow one from his teammates, requested the Rumanian Association not to count this Sweden-Rumania Team Match, they understood and agreed!

TYPES OF GRIP

Hand in hand with this discussion about the selection and care of your racket is how you're going to grip it. I mean, you've got to do that before you can execute the most basic of strokes, right? So again you've got to make a choice. The shakehands grip? Or the penholder grip? Which should it be? Or what possible variation of either?

The Shakehands Grip

''One gun is enough,'' advises the ''good'' bad gunslinger Shane (who plays to win) to his young pupil in that famous movie. And if you just think of uncurling your own trigger finger and extending it out along the bottom of your racket blade, while, keeping a good grip on your handle, you, friendly-like, greet your opponent with a ''Glad to

27

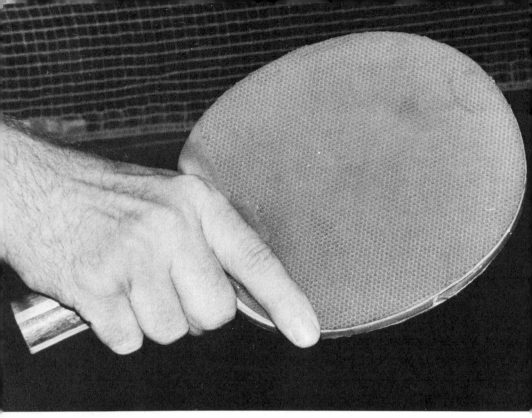

Shakehands grip (conventional forehand variation)—two views. (Pips-out racket.)

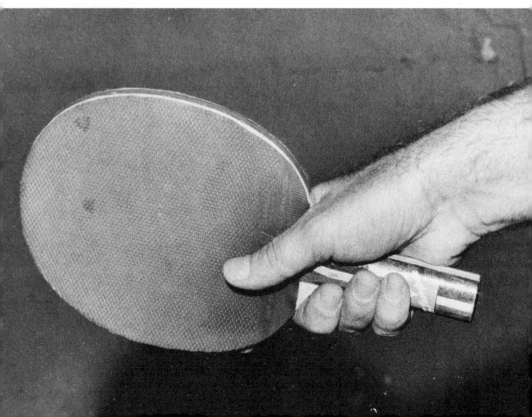

Shakehands grip (conventional forehand variation). (Pips-in racket.)

meetcha,'' you'll have a pretty good idea of the conventional shakehands grip.

Of course, since the great majority of Europeans and Americans have used this tennis grip for half a century, there are bound to be variations. Table tennis is a game for individuals, and so not unnaturally I myself use a grip that's a little different from the norm. My forefinger is not extended along the bottom of the blade but has moved up toward the center of the racket. To many people this looks strange, but although I didn't realize it when I first started out, I have very good precedents for steadying my racket so. The 1938 Czech World Champion Bohumil Vana had his trigger finger up toward the center this way and, 30 years later, the 1967 World Champion, Nobuhiko Hasegawa of Japan (who from the time he was a teenager, short in stature and needing extra leverage), had his forefinger centered even more—straight up the back of the blade, like an extension of the handle.

Today's two great Swedish stars, Stellan Bengtsson and Kjell

Johansson, use pretty much the same shakehands grip with the forefinger across the bottom of the blade but, while both employ the variation of keeping the thumb on the other side of the racket off the blade, Bengtsson has his thumb bent, pressing down on his middle finger, and Johansson has his stretched flat across, parallel to his forefinger. As for the legendary 4-time World Champion Richard Bergmann, his shakehands grip was similar to the Swedes' but with the variation that his thumb, the side of it (not the soft fleshy part), remained fairly centered on the bottom of the blade.

Some outstanding world-class players, like Laszlo Bellak, had very deceptive, non-tennislike grips and strokes. Learning the game in Hungary in the 1920s, "Laci" at first used only the backhand side of the wooden racket. In Bellak's shakehands variation, *two* fingers, both the forefinger and the middle finger, are side by side along the bottom of the blade, and the thumb on the other side of the racket has moved upright close to the side of the blade.

Sometimes a good player will play with a "cut handle" racket, one he's patiently whittled out, which he thinks will allow him to grip the handle better—perhaps so he won't continue to blister or otherwise put unwanted pressure on a finger. Other players will sand down the handle to make it lighter, will wrap it with heavy tape (I myself used to do this) for better balance (real or imagined), will put a non-slip grip on it, will even write a magical word or mantra on it ("Excalibur") that they hope will give them the racket power of King Arthur's sword.

Although obviously many variations in grip, eccentric or not, are possible, the whole point of using the shakehands as opposed to the penholder grip is to utilize both sides of your racket—especially the backhand side, for chopping, over-the-table volleying, or an on-the-run flick or pick-hit.

Therefore you must always be sure, if in hitting a forehand you've got your steadying forefinger up on the blade and suddenly you want or are forced to play a backhand, that you're not going to let the ball hit your finger. Which means, if you're like me, you'll quickly have to change from your forehand grip, drop that offending trigger finger down to its conventional position along the bottom of the blade, and simultaneously go into your backhand grip, move those curling fingers up close to the top of the handle, and get that steadying thumb up along the side of the

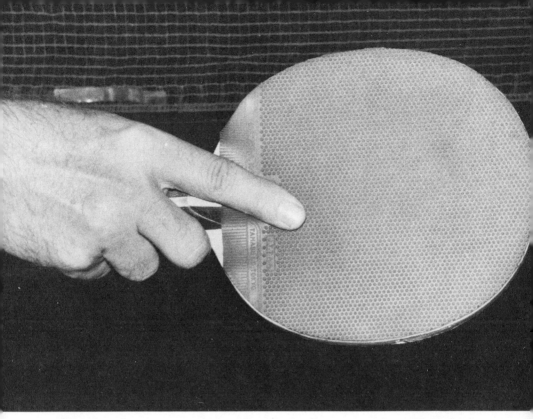

Shakehands grip (author's forehand variation)—two views. (Pips-out racket.)

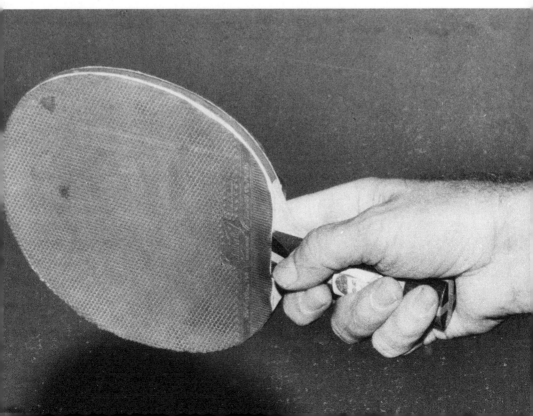

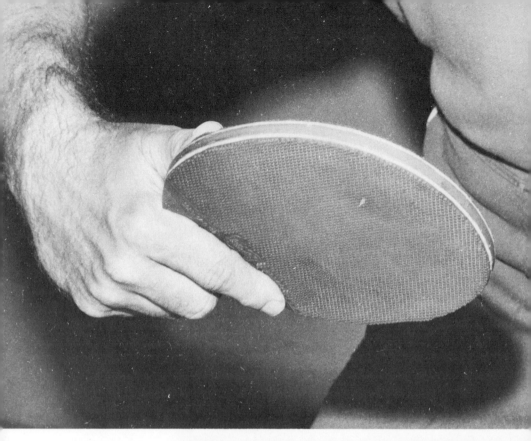

Shakehands grip (conventional backhand variation)—two views. (Pips-out racket.)

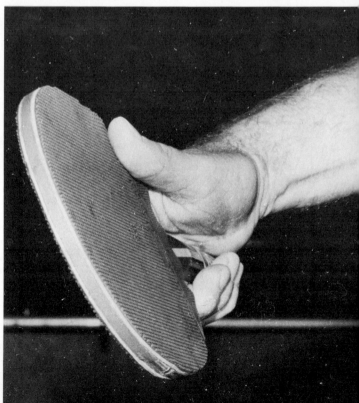

blade into its backhand-at-the-ready position. Bengtsson, Johansson, and most players, of course, with their standard grips, never have to worry about that forefinger, but though Vana and Hasegawa did, it didn't make them any less champions.

Practically any coach will tell you that whether you're going to be a penholder or a shakehands player you ought to grip the bat as close to the blade—indeed, the moving ball—as possible. The idea, everyone says, is to get the feel of playing with the blade rather than the handle. But while I hold the racket conventionally like this on my backhand side—my steady, controlling, blocking side, where my directing thumb up on the side of the blade acknowledges that "touch" and perfect racket angle are very, very important—I do *not* grip the bat close to the blade on my whip-it-in, point-winning forehand side.

No matter what anyone says, I've found I can get greater speed and wrist snap if I keep the strong, directing pressure on my forefinger, yet allow my fingers, my little finger and the one next to it particularly, which really hold the racket, to "slip" down until I have the very heel of the handle in the palm of my hand. With this grip and the right wrist snap, my ball goes in and I win the point. So that's good enough for me. There's no sense in copying others just to be copying, is there? Every real student I've ever had knows that.

Some coaches say you should hold the racket tightly, some say not too tightly, some say not tightly at all. Who, then, do you believe? Well, finally, you have to believe yourself. Obviously you don't want a cramp in your hand, but just as obviously if, say, like me, you're a blocker, there has to be a variable tension in your grip. How to handle your various opponents' slow rolls, drives, smashes, slow loops, fast loops? As you'll find out from experience, you can't possibly use the same light or firm touch to return each of these shots, differing as they do in their spin.

Also it's very possible, isn't it, that while you're at the ready position awaiting your opponent's serve, you're alert but relaxed, hands hanging gunslinger-capable but casual at your side. But then suppose you suddenly attack the serve. Quite clearly you're going to tighten your grip on the racket as you hit the ball. (Haven't you ever seen beginners at golf, especially women who are trying to be coached, who, after taking too long a backswing, relax as they come down into the

33

ball, and firm left hand and everything else goes loose and they lose all their power? Well, you don't want to do that.) So whether you hold the bat tightly or not depends on no hard and fast rule—it depends on you.

Naturally your at-the-ready stance, your footwork, your in-close or wide-ranging positional play—your style, in other words—all have a bearing on what grip you use. Is, for example, the double-wing shakehands player better able to handle balls that come deep on both sides of the table? Does he therefore not have to be as fast on his feet as a penholder who, taking the ball on one side of his racket only, has to "run around" his forehand? Can he then play competitive table tennis longer—into his 30s, 40s, 50s—than a penholder can? (Maybe some of you reading this book, who aren't yet and, oh, never will be, in near perfect physical condition, yet want to improve your play, are already 40 or over?) Does the shakehands player, as some say, have a center-line weakness where for a fraction of a second too long he cannot make up his mind whether to take the ball backhand or forehand?

These are rhetorical questions, which you can learn to answer for yourself. But already you must surely see that no racket, no grip, no style, is necessarily perfect. Of course you're going to understand much better what I've been saying in this general, preparatory way when in the next chapter I take you through the basic strokes and stances—then you're going to have to move and get the feel of the shots. For now, though, just see that if you use the shakehands grip it's not only got to feel comfortable to you, it's got to be very functional as well. I mean, mentally test yourself: for forehand shots, your forefinger is behind the ball; for backhand shots, your thumb is behind the ball. If you keep that continually in mind, the strokes will start to take care of themselves.

The Penholder Grip

I'm just not going to have nearly as much to say about the penholder grip as the shakehands, which, after all, is not only the grip I but the great majority of players in this country use. (Indeed, I get the impression that even more Asians are using it.) When I was in Japan in 1971, though, I saw high school kids with sleeping bags waiting in long lines to buy tickets for the World Championships. Many were reading a very

Chinese penholder Li Chen-shih preparing to topspin the ball. Note the head-down position of the racket and the thumb-and-forefinger grip. (Photo by Tommy Andersson)

fine, illustrative book on penholder (as well as shakehands) play by one of the greatest penholders, the former World Champion Ichiro Ogimura. So as I think of those kids all wanting to be like Ogimura, I'm sure that many coaches are correct in saying that the penholder grip, which we in our tennis-oriented U.S. are conditioned to find awkward, but which I'm using now in first writing out these pages in longhand, is just as natural as shaking hands or pointing a gun —especially of course for Orientals who from a very early age in their imaginations have gotten quite a bit of over-the-table practice with white rice and chopsticks.

Many coaches also say that for hitting the forehand the penholder grip is *more* natural because the racket is already in its proper head-

35

Three-time World Champion Chuang Tse-tung and another, back-of-the-racket, view of the penholder grip. (Photo by Dean Johnson)

down position, ready to be brought upward and forward in a forehand attack. They argue that shakehands players like myself have to use a short, clockwise stroke just to get the head down before whipping it back up to achieve a similar snap effect. And, I agree, this is true. But—what can I tell you?—though I play a penholder, close-to-the-table blocking and hitting style, I've always felt much more comfortable with the shakehands bat, have always thought I could target my dreams with it.

Also, I'm absolutely convinced from watching the best players in the world that one grip is really no better or worse than the other. It so happens that my table tennis life has been spent playing shakehands against

36

shakehands players—and so you'll get the benefit of that background. But if I'd been born Chinese and were writing this book primarily for penholders, it would have amounted to much the same thing: anyone reading this, if he works hard enough, can become a winner.

When I first started to play seriously, good players, isolated over here from the great Asian stars, told me that penholders couldn't hit backhands. But in 1971 when I saw Chuang Tse-tung at the end of his career move so quickly, so smoothly, I saw how wrong they were. He snapped in balls with his backhand that the best players in the world sometimes couldn't even get their rackets on.

Others argue that the shakehands player deceptively gets to use two different kinds of rubber and deceptively twirl the racket—as if, compared to the penholder, he had two bats to the other's one. But it's just as Shane said, "One gun is as good as two"—and there's no spin answer, once you catch on to it, to the fast-draw kill shot.

Of course, if the very fast penholder doesn't outdraw his powerful opponent and is caught back from the table awkwardly trying to block or retrieve, he's dead. Unless . . . unless by what seems like magic (whoever said penholders can't chop?), he's back there defending deliberately, like the great Chang Shih-lin, 1971 World Mixed Doubles Champion, mixing up his opponents with his ever-changing, ever-returning spin.

So, all right, shakehands or penholder—you make up your mind. But here's a little tip for you. Before you go making any drastic changes in what you find an instinctively satisfying (but strangely not a winning) game, you'd better be sure to ask yourself, "Have I really been watching the ball?"

TYPES OF BALL

I'm not going into any prolonged discussion here about the ball, the table, the lighting, the floor—in short, the playing conditions of any particular court, which are always of extreme importance to the very best players. I assume you're going to a club to begin taking on better competition, and that at this club you'll find at least adequate playing conditions.

But for any son or father who is at first a little reluctant to come up out

1971 World Mixed Doubles Champion Chang Shih-lin. Who said penholders can't hit backhands?

of that basement game room into the real world of the sport, I'd just like to mention, before I discuss the kind of ball you ought to be playing with (under naturally the best kind of over-the-table lighting possible), a few words about the table and the floor on which you're playing.

First, the table. Does it warp? Do its edges splinter? Is there a glare on the surface? Does the table paint come off on the ball? Does the ball bounce uniformly? And in connection with the table, the floor. Is it wooden or concrete or what? Whatever it is, it will affect the bounce on the table—make it slower or faster and thus give an advantage or disadvantage, say, to the spinner. For example, on a hard floor, the ball is more apt to shoot off the table, to slide, so that if you're a blocker it will become more difficult for you to get the height you need to block your opponent's shot back.

As the bounce changes with tables and floors, the more so does it, of course, with the ball. So different is the bounce of even the best balls available that I've had good players call me not just weeks but months ahead of time to try to find out what ball is going to be used in a major tournament, so that they might begin right away practicing to get used to it. "If you loop or smash this ball hard," I've heard one of our best players say of even a USTTA-approved ball, "it goes right down. It's so soft and light, it doesn't bounce through, doesn't come up to you."

For what it's worth to you, then (and to me it's worth only as little

Jack Howard (left) and Dal Joon Lee ready to test balls prior to their match for the U.S. Open at Hofstra University, Long Island, New York, March, 1972. (Photo by Mal Anderson)

or as much as the truth), I feel I must tell you that most professional players think the Nittaku ball is best—and so of course I recommend it to you. Most balls everywhere are awful. And this is too bad, for in the beginning, while you're learning your strokes, the quality of the ball is more important than the quality of the racket.

If you can't buy a Nittaku, test out what you can get. Spin the ball—like a little top on a table. Is it wobbly? How does it feel? Is it so soft you can push your thumb into it?

I once accompanied a famous player into a big sporting goods store in a large city—where, eventually, he got around to asking about balls. The salesman went over, opened a large box behind the counter, then another, smaller one, and finally came back with a ball. Which my friend, on testing, in a calm, deliberate rage pushed his thumb through.

"It's obviously unplayable," he said in a very pleasant voice.

The salesman was shocked. "Hey," he said, "I just opened a new gross of those balls. You didn't have to do that."

But my proud friend, I knew, *did* have to do that. It was as basic to him, his needs, his long, too-long-unrecognized life in table tennis as even the tired feeling of joy in executing the most elementary of shots is to a great champion.

chapter three

Half a dozen years or so ago, two of the greatest Japanese champions were being asked questions in a "New Year's Interview" somewhere in Japan. "What's your hobby?" said the interviewer to World Champion Hasegawa. "Nothing," answered Hasegawa—"table tennis only." Then the interviewer turned to Kohno, World Runner-up Finalist to Hasegawa, and asked, "If you could have any life-course other than table tennis, what would it be?" To which Kohno replied, "I can't think of another life-course."

As I move through this first chapter on basic strokes, I'm going to pretend that you have at least something of a champion's desire—for, believe me, I could wish for nothing more important in a pupil than that. I'm also going to assume that you are either just learning to play or that you are already an enthusiast who's looking to pick up a few

basic strokes I

pointers on how better to teach the game to a good friend who can share in your fun.

BACKHAND BLOCK

I'm starting you off with the backhand shots first—particularly the block, because this stroke will right away give you some ''feel'' of the table and because it demands of you a knack, a ''touch,'' for not only solidly repelling but also aggressively directing that ball that the obviously experienced player opposite you (like me, say) in the beginning has control of.

Learning the block shot first will give you some much-needed confidence, will offer you a psychological advantage over those who begin in some other way. If you can learn to block decently (and, as I know from teaching lots of students, you can—very quickly) you'll not only be able to shield yourself from your attacker, hold your vantage point up close to the table, but will be able, by deflecting the ball in various directions, to learn to maneuver your way around. After you can place your block where you want it, the next step is simple: you learn how to follow with an attack of your own.

As in other self-assertive sports that stress individual combat and are therefore so appealing to people fast of foot, hand, and eye (I think particularly, though not exclusively, of Orientals), the idea is to let your opponent use his force against himself. The harder he swings (and of course follows through), the faster the ball rebounds, comes back at or away from him, off your skillfully angled racket. Often your opponent has not regained, and never will be able to regain, his balance to follow up the advantage that once was his but is his no longer.

I want you now to take up in your shakehands grip the racket you've comfortably selected for your learning sessions—the one with the pips out on one side, the pips in on the other. You should stand directly behind the center line of the table while your friendly opponent topspins, spins the ball towards you, easy, casually, over and over again down the center line, directly at what in the beginning will be easier for you to handle, your soft rubber pips-out side.

Your stance, the at-the-ready position of your racket, your free left hand (I'm assuming you're right-handed; lefties, sorry, you'll always have to reverse), your grip, and the changing angle of your racket are all very important. In trying to teach some kids in the Long Island schools these past few years I've been struck by how awkwardly they initially stand at the table—it's as if they've never seen any good players and consequently haven't the slightest idea what to do. Any beginner who wants to get good at any sport must have an active imagination, must be able to see at least the big stars.

As you ready yourself for play, you're in a semi-crouch, your knees are bent, and your feet are not precisely squared but are in a slightly open stance. Your weight is evenly distributed, mostly on the balls of your feet (but neither heel is up). It's important that you have the sense of leaning over the table—because of course you are going to block the ball immediately after it hits your side. I have to stress that word "immediately" because the whole secret to blocking well is to "trap" the ball the split second after it hits the table, before it has a chance to hop too high or too much to the side and so get by you.

With the shakehands grip you're using (it would have been the same had you been born a penholder), the racket is not in an upright, lollipop position (beginners often have this mistaken tendency to want to swat the ball). Instead, the racket is turned to the side—with the duck-bill handle of the face blade to the right, parallel to the end line. The blade is centered above the white line, about 6 inches in over the table, as if, were you to set the racket down, you could balance it straight up on its side.

Now as your playing partner (call him a coach, if you want), topspins the ball at your racket, you do nothing. That is, you apply no directing force whatsoever of your own—but just hold the bat steady and very carefully watch your opponent's ball hit it and very carefully watch how the ball that has just been topspinning towards you now rebounds off your racket and comes back pretty much up the center of the table and rather high to your opponent.

As you continue watching the ball and even begin to feel some control in doing this simple exercise, take the initiative, suggest that your partner deliberately miss your racket so that you will be forced to move the target a little left, a little right—in that way, the ever-changing center of your blade will better meet the ball. Also, as you begin to feel some sense of rhythm, bring your left hand up and out—as if it too had a balancing racket.

Your forefinger should be along the bottom of the blade, your other three fingers curled around the top of the handle, and your thumb on its side should be near the edge of your racket to provide steadiness. This thumb is very important, for, as you may now experiment, it will help you, as you slightly turn your wrist, to "close" your paddle, tilt the bat in toward the net more. Now, as you'll soon see, you'll be returning the ball lower over the net. It follows then that the more the ball is topspinning at you, the more your racket must be closed to keep your return down.

Thus far of course you've been on the defensive. But keep practicing —your time will come. Be steady, steady, steady. Keep returning the ball as straight as you can and tilt your racket in. As your experienced

Three-time U.S. Champion Patty Martinez. Hand up behind her—as if to say, "Don't bother me. I've got it all together. This is how to block." (Photo by Mal Anderson)

Tim Boggan, 1974 U.S. and Canadian Open Seniors Champion, demonstrating his catch-the-ball-at-the-center-of-you block. (Photo by Mal Anderson)

partner begins more and more to vary his play from that white center line into your backhand box and then back to the center line again, you will have to continue to keep your weight evenly distributed and your bat centered over your midsection, will have to, in taking short little steps to your left and to your right, be aware of the increasing importance of good footwork.

After a while, though your coach has more and more changed the pace of his fast, medium, and slow topspin, and though sometimes his balls come back deeper on the table than at other times, you continue to watch the ball beautifully and are undeniably returning shot after shot, are actually containing your aggressive friend.

So, all right, still keeping your left hand out for balance, try yourself now to direct the ball from one side of the table to the other, though not naturally with any force of your own. Bring your racket a little left, a little right, always stopping it to hold steady as the ball comes to meet it, always trapping the ball the split second it bounces. It may be, too, that if you block the ball not precisely in the center of the blade but a little more toward the handle of your racket you'll have more control.

Gradually you'll get better at anticipating both where you have to intercept your opponent's ball and where you want to place your return. Later, you may turn the racket head from its squared-off position a little, or even, on certain sophisticated occasions, a lot. Still later, as you become more and more consistent with your timing to the point where you scarcely ever miss returning the ball, you may, by changing your stroke slightly, even combine a little deadening chop with your no-spin block. But here in the beginning just concentrate on being relentlessly steady.

O.K., O.K., I know you're getting tired of just neutralizing your friend's topspin with your own no-spin shots. I know you're just dying to hit the ball, so go ahead. Smack some in any old way. Your friend understands. He'll set a few up, go chase the ball, keep you as happy as he can. He wants you to have fun. Then, after you've recovered your patience, have gotten that desire to smash momentarily out of your system, and have resharpened your blocking touch, he'll feel that you're ready to learn the next basic in-close-to-the-table defensive shot—the push.

BACKHAND PUSH

In learning the block, you've started out being somewhat passive. But, be patient, the more you learn, the more active, even aggressive, you'll soon be. Go back now to the ready position behind the center line you were in when you first started practicing the block. Keep the same crouching stance and the same thumb-up-to-the-side-of-the-blade grip. But instead of just holding the face of your racket steady as your opponent topspins fairly hard at you, push it, without tilting it, squarely towards the ball, straight up the line about a foot or so. Then do the same thing left and right.

It should be clear that your force, added to your opponent's, is too great. You immediately begin pushing the ball off the table. And when you close your racket to lower the trajectory of your return and then push straight out, that's not much good either. You don't have the control you had before when you just held the racket steady. That is, since you don't know consciously yet how to use your wrist to come up over the ball with topspin, you're mostly jabbing the ball every which way, often into the net.

So this push shot—what's it supposed to do for you and how does it work?

Well, what happens if you open the racket, tilt it back towards you, much as if it were a plate? That's absurd, you say. Obviously the ball will go way up. True, but if you and your opponent make an adjustment or two, it won't.

Drop about a foot back from your in-over-the-table block position and understand that with this new stroke you don't want to trap the ball but expect to catch it with your racket just after it comes off the top of its bounce. Of course you're about to see in a moment that this time your mirror image, your opponent, isn't going to be topspinning, but, don't worry, you'll soon grasp what's expected of you.

Take up your racket on its squared-off edge, as you did for the block, then tilt the blade open, but only about halfway back to the extremely flat plate position. Now, keeping your wrist firm throughout, bring the racket straight back to the umbilical center of you, and, in one continuous, fluid movement, push the blade steadily forward and a little downward right out into the bottom half of the oncoming ball and

47

Swedish-coached Elsie Spinning of the U.S. showing the backhand push. Many players prefer the right foot in front of the left one even if they're in close to the table.

In U.S.-China matches at Long Island's Nassau Coliseum, April, 1972, three-time U.S. Champion Bernie Bukiet (right) plays against a Chinese penholder who has his own way of pushing the ball. (Photo by Mal Anderson)

straight through back up the center line. Since your open blade provides underspin, and since your partner is pushing with you, the ball will stay down.

Practice pushing the ball left and right and back to the center again. Be sure that you keep your left hand up for balance. And that you watch the ball very carefully throughout. Your experienced partner is going to continue to push with you—but never to your forehand side. The forehand push is used more than the forehand block, but, since I'm looking for you right from the go to attack when the ball comes over on the forehand side (which, I know, I know, exasperatingly it hasn't yet), I don't want to take it up just now.

All right, you're keeping to that backhand grip and you're leaning forward, pushing perhaps more aggressively than you were before, trying to keep the ball as low as you can over the net. Sometimes, as your partner deliberately pushes long, you'll need to back up a little; other times, as he pushes short, you'll need to come in a little. Hence the need for you always to be taking tiny, turning steps, the better to keep the ball centered in front of you so you'll always have a chance to control the table. Later, you'll be looking to hit or loop off the push and then your anticipation and positioning will be even more important. The one most important thing to remember in all of this is to keep moving and never be caught flat-footed reaching for a ball.

Floating the Ball

O.K., so far so good. Now I want you to move back four or five feet from the table and, while your opponent topspins, continue pushing —or rather concentrate on what I'm going to call "floating" the ball. Right away you'll see you'll have to make an adjustment or two. Since you're not up close to the table, you'll have to adopt much more of a sideways than a squared-off stance. Make sure that your right foot is pointing tablewards and that your left one is back and to the side. This will allow you to take the necessary longer backswing.

Then, instead of taking the racket back to your midsection, you bring it over and up to about shoulder height, then forward and down, then smoothly through. Notice that it's best, even if you have to take a step or two up, a step back, to let the ball slow down and fall about waist-high.

As you practice shifting your weight and moving your feet, you're beginning to prepare yourself for making the stronger defensive stroke of chopping the ball (a subject I'm going to concern myself with in the next chapter). About this time, too, whether you're pushing from in close against another push or floating the ball from afar against topspin, you might be aware that, whenever you don't follow absolutely straight through (which is almost always), you've picked up, deliberately or accidentally, some sidespin in your stroke. You might see, for instance, that if you push straight out and then counterclockwise, trying to keep the ball and your "feel" for it on the racket longer, you've got both underspin and right-to-left sidespin into the shot—a combination that might on occasion provide you with an advantage.

Later, you may decide that the best stance for you, whether you're pushing up close or from farther out, is the one in which your right foot is always in front of your left one. Why? Because later if you're looking to loop off the push you can quickly drop this right foot over sideways and back of the left one and be in immediate position to topspin a forehand. Now, though, since you won't be much of a winner back there floating the ball, I'm going to get you up to the table again where perhaps you'll learn to be much more aggressive.

BACKHAND ROLL, DRIVE, FLICK, SMASH

The next backhand shot I want you to experiment with here is the backhand roll. Your obliging opponent is going to continue pushing the ball—but altogether away from the center line, exclusively into the middle of your backhand box. You've therefore moved over to try some topspin shots yourself.

Your grip and shoulders-forward stance remain the same, but you're about a foot and a half back and of course to the left of your original up-close blocking position at the center line. Your racket is not now squared-off but closed, tilted towards the net. Later you'll learn about trying to disguise its intentions. Your balancing left hand is at the ready too—all it needs is a racket.

As your opponent pushes the ball, you start your backswing, bring the racket head up from just above your crotch, up and over the ball, swinging your wrist easy as you follow the thumb on your bat through into your opponent's backhand court. Up and over. Up and over. Up and over. And as you come through, your left heel goes up and the weight shifts over to the ball of your right foot. This is a simple, old-fashioned shot, the antithesis of which today is World Champion Jonyer's backhand loop (which I'll have a few words to say about in the advanced play chapter), but it's a good stroke to use to teach a beginner about topspin. Also, if you compare it to its accelerated twin brother, the drive, it may serve as a reminder here to others that changes of spin and speed on shots can be stroked much the same way.

Your backhand backswing, remember, is much shorter than your forehand swing, and so it's very easy for someone with a squared-off stance, even though he's just learning the game, to hit through the ball quickly. One can quickly understand how to use more wrist, smoothly snap through the forearm, and so, keeping the elbow upright, even further shorten his backswing.

51

Sweden's Hans Alser in a 1968 sequence showing an easy "up and over" backhand. (Photo sequence by Mal Anderson)

52

This quick stroke, executed without the need for any tip-off positioning on your part, is particularly good for catching an opponent off guard or (strategically just the opposite) for backhand countering —where, as is more and more common today, you and your opponent are each fighting for control of the table and neither wants to give the other a forehand opening. Of course the closer the player is in toward the net, the less follow-through action is necessary.

The counterdrive stroke, then, which is really sort of a topspin block, need not have so upright a follow-through—indeed, might even on occasion be as flat as a turned-over plate. Five-time World Champion Victor Barna had a backhand flick that he used to incomparable advantage by beginning his stroke even as the ball was starting to rise from the table. Instead of coming up on it, he hit it with a straight bat in a straight-line return. Most players though, often defensive players who come running in close to the net, flick in a loose high ball (from an opponent's bad drop shot, perhaps)—hit it in about chest high with a short, quick stroke.

The backhand smash, however (the most difficult power shot in all of table tennis), is a bit more complicated. You have to anticipate the right ball, then do a little two-step or Japanese jump to get into the right position. Your left foot is back and opened to the side, while your right foot is forward, leading the way. The up-and-over stroke is pretty much as before, except now you have more room to move the racket back and through with all the weight of the waist-turn coming onto the ball of the right foot. According to penholder Chuang Tse-tung, who, as it turned out, was not perfect after all, his steadying thumb should not have been used to try to supply extra power, for it only interfered with his important wrist action.

Since I'm not writing this book solely for the beginner rooted to any time or place, I want to add some further, and in some instances modifying, comments to those I've already made about the backhand.

The more modern stance is often to keep the left foot forward a little, for today the backhand is rarely, if at all, going to be swept back and fully through—powered over to the diagonal—as it was in the old days with Barna and others. Today, people say, the time for that stroke is gone. Against a fast blocker particularly, the player has only a split second to return to his ready position. Therefore the emphasis is on

Charlie Wuvanich, world-class player and coach, finishing a short-stroked backhand down the center line.

speed, and the backhand is not an all-out kill but is hit very fast up the opponent's forehand side or up the middle.

The at-the-ready racket position for the backhand should be high, not (as it was taught years ago, and I think still ought to be taught, to beginners) low and then brought up. In the speeded-up '70s, the argument goes, you can't afford to make two movements when one will do.

The racket hand is held like a mask over the heart, like an illusionist palming a card, with the wrist kept steady, then flipped over and out. Milan Orlowski, the great Czech player, who uses pips out on his backhand, doesn't bring his hand back at all. His four *fingers* go back, while his wrist holds firm, then the stroke is snapped deceptively through, in one direction or the other. Against a chop to the backhand, the player bends down and, with his racket like an overturned plate, lifts up and over and out.

With the pips-out rubber, when you don't topspin the ball but block it in a straight motion back to your opponent, the ball will have backspin on it. If your masked hand blocks the ball up and down in a fast motion, a stroke I often use, it will have no spin on it at all.

The backhand, which I've deliberately taken up before the forehand, is very important, for, unless you're an exceptional player like Surbek, if you don't have one, you can't hope to quickly maneuver the ball (later you'll see why that right foot is already behind the left one) to set up your point-winning forehand. Johansson is known for his pounding "hammer" shots—but it's his steady, all-controlling backhand that prepares him to make his leaping forehand kills.

A much-talked-about example of a player's backhand failing or deserting him can be seen in, of all people, that heretofore ideal model for all players, the 1971 World Champion Stellan Bengtsson. Zlatko Cordas, the world-class Yugoslav who is now the National Coach of Canada, was telling me recently that Bengtsson, for some unclear reason, is not playing his backhand as strongly in 1975 as he was in 1971. It used to be that you had to rush against Bengtsson, for if you ever put, say, three balls in a row to his backhand (to keep him from getting forehand control), he would always anticipate that strategy by hitting a backhand hard that would enable him to take control from that side of the table, too. Suddenly, though, in backhand-to-backhand play with opponent after opponent, he's stopped hitting that backhand shot and so, subject to this fatal flaw, is not as great as he was before.

Of course, he's recognized the problem. Sometimes, in an effort to avoid being contained on that backhand side by an opponent who now has time to wait for the right moment to get in an aggressive shot of his own, Bengtsson moves too early to try to run around his backhand side to hit the ball with his forehand—at which point his opponent simply fast blocks the ball far over to Bengtsson's forehand side. Perhaps the young Swede's solution to losing his once very effective backhand is to come up with another?

1971 World Singles Champion Stellan Bengtsson demonstrating his steady backhand. (Photo by Mike Hoffland)

FOREHAND DRIVE

So far, you've learned to put no spin, underspin, sidespin, and topspin on the ball—without changing your grip and (though you were never stationary) without moving too much. That's a beginning.

Now I want to show you what to do when the ball comes to your pips-out forehand. (That's right, turn over the racket—you've been playing with the pips out on your backhand. I ask you now, though, to use and continue using the pips out on your forehand until I get into discussing the loop.) I'm going to begin by teaching you the stroke I learned to play with back in the old hard rubber bat days—and which I still use to win many a match today. If you want to learn it, with or without its eccentricities, fine; if not, that's O.K., too. For soon, maybe even with the help of my son Scott, who as I write this is just about due back from a table tennis training camp, I'll move on into the more modern ways of hitting forehands—which, you know how it goes, in time won't seem so modern.

The first thing you have to do is change from your backhand to your forehand grip. The steadying thumb on the side drops down to wherever you want it—on the racket or off. And then if, like me, you have an unusual place for that forefinger, up on the blade, you'll have to get it there.

To begin with, your partner, your mirror image across from you, is going to oblige by blocking to your forehand while you topspin, stroke up and over the ball.

At the forehand court ready position for this initial lesson, you have an open stance in that your left foot is just left of, and pointing a little into, the center line of the table (were that line painted on the floor), while your right foot is behind, big toe pointing in another imaginary line to the right diamond edge of the table. As you prepare to come forward and upward into the ball, your weight shifts from your right foot onto your left one, which has led you into the shot. Naturally, after following through (it may be you'll come completely off your right foot), you must quickly rebalance your weight into the ready position.

In the beginning, the bottom edge of your blade may be squared off on that imaginary line from your big toe, so that your racket faces your opponent's forehand court. However, don't feel that you have to be so mechanical about this—it's quite possible that even as you wait for the serve, both your racket and your balancing free hand are down at your sides, gunslinger-like, to fast draw. I myself prefer my hands triangular-like so much over my center that sometimes as I wait for the serve my balancing left hand even holds the blade.

The racket head is not brought back so simply as it was on the backhand side. I open the blade and bring the lollipop face down and around and up—like a long thin U. And then as I come up from under the table with all this generated topspin into the ball, I turn my wrist, or don't turn it, depending on the direction I want to send the ball, and snap as I make contact—after which my forearm follow-through, which is short, sends the ball downward.

In copying this swing you're thus making the outline of a stroke not so different from the handle of the racket you're holding: down and up—and sometimes a little snap curve to the left. You'll notice too that the penholder, because of his grip, already has his racket head down, so that he needs only to bring it up and snap through.

My free left hand is both outstretched and curled, as if on the follow-through I were holding a bow with it. It's a good idea, by the way, to try to have a mental picture of what you look like playing. To that end, it may help you to find a metaphor for your stroke, as I have for mine.

I have something of a peculiar grip. The controlling forefinger of my racket hand is up on the back of the blade just to the right of center, and my handle-gripping little finger and the one next to it are way down at the bottom of the handle that is tucked into my palm. When I come up through the ball and make my snap contact at the height of the bounce, my middle finger, which is up close to the top of the handle where it "should" be, pushes up against the blade (for 17 years I've always had a callous there) and, as I follow straight up through in the precise direction I've aimed, my thumb and forefinger end up in parallel pointing position, almost as if they too were curled and I was holding a bowstring up there by my left eye.

As I'm ready to fire my shot, my weight is not at all exclusively on my leading left foot, for I'm arched up on the tiptoes of my right foot. And as I come through the ball, I push off on those toes. Then, as I pivot, my right foot swivels around and follows the direction of my pointing forefinger and thumb, so that I feel bow-and-arrow all in a direct firing line downward, following the lead of my left shoulder.

In addition to those still-exciting peculiarities that I year after year conform to, I have one other unique stroking habit—and that is my so-called "no look" forehand. Which is the forehand I've just de-

58

scribed to you—except that, whereas my body is positioned so that my follow-through is expected to go straight up the center line or even, if I move my bow, cross court (in which case my kill shot has left-to-right sidespin), it really goes to my opponent's backhand. Why? Because at the last second, as my paddle accelerates through, I turn my wrist over and, head still down looking at the spot where I made contact (as in golf) I hook the ball sharply in to that side.

Actually, there's method to my madness, for when I snap my wrist like that at the last moment, there's quite a margin for error and an exaggerated follow-through for this variation of my stroke is quite reasonable and necessary. The shot is made even more deceptive because, wanting to attack, I've been running around my forehand so often (in this way I'm like a penholder), I've practically perfected this forehand shot from my backhand side, and, though I've scarcely any room down the backhand line, I still unexpectedly hook it in there.

Although I like to hit my shot in hard, like spectacularly to ''pass'' my opponent, I often, if I have the positional advantage, don't have to risk doing that, for even if the other player, surprised, caught off balance because of his conditioned anticipation over the years, manages to return even my medium-hit shot, I'll surely be able to move fast enough to really kill the next one with a no-look. Of course, in the most important sense, it's not a ''no-look'' forehand I hit in at all. In fact, quite the contrary. I watch the ball much better than most hitters do because my style encourages me to.

At any rate, my forehand, if I can get a chance to hit it, is a very potent weapon. I can send the ball left, right, or center and almost always without my opponent's being able to judge for sure where it's going. I therefore try to commit myself at just about every opportunity (like the Chinese penholder hitters) to be very aggressive, even attempting to hit in serve after serve and trying with my own serve and follow-up to quickly end the point. In hoping to take the initiative this way before the looper can get to spinning, I'm paradoxically a very modern player.

Naturally most of my opponents want to play me aggressively. That is, all but the very best defenders, who, having played me enough, are not fooled by my deception (they've spotted little telltale signs that others, even I, haven't? If they have, they don't tell me), or who, be-

60

cause they're back farther from the table, have more time to get to my ball as it falls.

What has made my style so successful against other hitters, however, is the fact that I am one of the very best blockers in the country. And so, as long as I have fast hands and feet, my forehand game can't be easily neutralized even with my opponent's repeated attacks to my backhand.

After you've gotten the hang of this "U" of a stroke—and that of course means hours of practice—remember to keep your left hand up for balance. And as you swing through, make sure that your racket head down-and-up-and-in stroke is made rather close to your body. At one time I used to play with a handkerchief under my arm. If it didn't fall, I'd know that over and over again I'd be at least trying to make the same free, elbow-in (but, careful, not too in) stroke. (Whether, too cautious, you can always keep from "tightening," from changing your stroke so that you're incorrectly "steering" the ball, as you feel the mounting pressure in an important game, is another matter.)

I've used this very durable, rather representative swing of mine

THE BOGGAN "NO-LOOK" FOREHAND. (Facing page, top) Though his head remains fixed even after he makes contact with the ball (compare a golfer following through, then looking up to watch his shot), the author's got off a normal topspin shot without any last-minute hook or twist of the racket. (Facing page, center) This picture complements the first one. The hitter's head disconcertingly still hasn't moved by the time the ball has reached the net—but, again, the ball goes where it's expected to, to the opponent's backhand. (Facing page, bottom) This time the racket head has been twisted, and because the opponent's high ball has originally gotten a little behind the hitter, here's what the opponent confusingly sees—the hitter's head turned even more away from him. (Below) This picture complements the third one. It shows what the opponent doesn't see until it's too late—the ball hit deceptively not to his backhand but, just the opposite, down his forehand line.

61

since watching the best hard rubber bat players in the '50s. But my follow-through is not as long as most of theirs was because in the last 10 years that I've been back playing again, the sponge rubber revolution has made the game faster, so that after you hit your shot you have to move more quickly than ever before to get back into your potential point-winning position again for your opponent's return.

Which reminds me that I'd better get back to working very specifically on your forehand. Your playing partner wants you to move to the center of the table while he blocks balls directly at you that you are to continue topspinning—right now just to his center. Occasionally, he'll block balls to your right, which will demand not that you reach for the ball but that you take a little one-step over (left foot, right foot) and then ("Don't let the ball get behind you!"), after you learn that shot, another little one-step (left foot, right foot—I always move my left foot first) back into your ready position again. Then he will move you over to your backhand box, where, with all the initial symmetry of chess, you will hit forehands to his backhand box. When, however, he puts that occasional ball out beyond the reach of your forehand, you will have to take not just one little (left, right) step but two. And then the two little steps back.

It may be that after more and more practice, and particularly from your opponent's body position and his hand and wrist movement, you can anticipate taking those necessary little steps a split second earlier than you did before. The more you see that in an actual game the ball isn't going to be coming right at you, the more you may agree with Hasegawa's line about footwork being the "life" of his professional table tennis, for when that goes, everything goes.

Your playing partner now wants you to go back to your at-the-ready position for the forehand and wants you to start whipping his blocks in again. But this time, as he accommodatingly, precisely, blocks, he wants you to gradually move your way, still hitting forehands to his racket, over to your backhand court. And then, still hitting forehands, gradually come back to your beginning position. Of course, he's moving too. And, in fact, may have you take over his blocking role so you'll be feeding his forehand for a while. Which means you'll have to change your grip again. Still, it only takes a mini-second, right? You might even be able to do it while playing a point.

It's very important, right from the start, to see yourself and the player opposite you as complementary figures, as mirror images. Because the more you understand and anticipate your opponent's actions, the more deeply you'll understand your own. What is my opponent trying to do? What am I trying to do? What does he expect me to do? What do I expect him to do? And thinking so, just as in life—in bridge or poker or chess—the deception that complicates and makes the game more fun is suddenly upon you.

But in the beginning it's no fun fooling someone who's just learning. So here's a point. Your back and forth travel along the edge of the table has shown you that it's much more comfortable for any hitter, yourself included now, to have more of an ''open'' table to hit to. It was a good thing—while you were over there on your forehand side, your opponent was nice and suddenly didn't block one far to your left. If, however, you're on your backhand side and your opponent blocks it far to your right, you can still fast step over there and hit the ball in—maybe even where he isn't expecting you to, right up the line opposite, into his backhand. I mean, if you can hit the ball straight up the center line, why can't you hit it up any line of your own making? Why, if it comes cross court, do you have to hit it back in the same predictable cross-court way? You don't want to be just a pattern player, do you?

Forehand Block

What's more, it's as if your opponent approved of self-analysis and knew something of what you were thinking. For, after you've again picked the right ball to topspin through, he surprises you with a change in pattern. Just as you think you're going to win a point, he unexpectedly, mildly, counters your topspin with a topspin of his own over into your far forehand. Caught off guard, off balance, you instinctively, quickly, stick the forehand face of your racket out in that squared-off, partially closed position you learned how to backhand block with —and, sure enough, the ball hits the racket squarely and rebounds back over the net to where your equally surprised opponent doesn't even get his racket on the ball.

Generally speaking, this forehand block is a very temporizing, though sometimes very accurate, shot for when you can't counter, or for when you're on the defensive, or when you're off balance and try-ing to move into another position that will allow you to recover control of the table.

So you've learned through trial and error that you prefer a ready position that gives you more open table. You're not as young maybe and certainly not as anticipatory or as fast yet as an experienced penholder who, bat head down at the ready, just loves to hit forehands and so stands way over to his backhand diamond-point edge to receive. But you're slowly getting the picture. "O.K.," says your experienced playing partner opposite, "now that you've found your at-the-ready spot, let's see what you can do. I'll defend; you hit."

You stand a little left of center behind your backhand box and, with your forehand grip, are waiting to be fed shots to topspin. The ball is coming up high (but not too high), you've no trouble adjusting your swing, your timing, to the ball's speed and spin—in short, you're doing just fine. Indeed, you're beginning to claim, if not yet a trophy, at least your reward for being patient, for persevering. As your inde-fatigable ball-chasing partner keeps putting up shots for you to hit, you're whipping the ball through with more and more boldness, are pretty soon actually slamming in outright point winners. Wow, you don't know about your partner, but you can't get enough of this prac-tice. (Oh, that's the hardest part of being a teacher—chasing those balls while you're building up your pupil's confidence, his ego.)

After a while, with more and more practice, you can even whip the ball down your opponent's forehand line. Which of course is risky be-cause you don't have as much room there to get the ball on the table, but which offers the advantage of drawing your opponent away from his set position diagonally across from you so you might follow up with a shot to his backhand. As, in fact or fantasy, you pass him with such a shot, one that he can't even get his racket on, he can only smile and say, "Got me that time! Nice combination." Which of course pleases you very much. What fun this game is, you think—and not so hard after all.

In time, though, the ball is not coming to you as high as it was be-fore, and now you're having more than a little difficulty "lifting" it. There must be something on it. Some sort of extra spin. As you play on, you try making your U swing a little longer, your follow-through a little faster. Whenever a high one (but not too high) comes in, you topspin it fine, but, because even your own topspin is bringing the ball down, that low floater (perhaps even with a touch of chop?) is giving you trouble. You wish you could wait for the right high ball.

Your partner, seeing that you're mentally a little tired, urges you to take over his role of varying the height of this floater return. But to your surprise he soon reflects an unexpected image—begins floating the ball with you, or, more accurately with the little move-in-close adjustment he has you make, begins pushing with you again.

Then, adjusting to your rhythms, anticipating when you're about to put one ball up rather higher than another, he suddenly takes a little one-step or—it seems so quick—maybe even a two-step over and topspins a ball at you that catches you a little unaware. As you continue varying your high or low push to his forehand, center, and backhand, you see that sooner or later he has no trouble changing from his backhand to his forehand grip and, because his footwork is so good, can topspin a forehand (not to say a backhand) from anywhere.

Now he asks you to try what he's doing. He positions you at the center line and starts slowly pushing with you down the center line, keeping the ball low. Then he says, "When I count 3 you change your grip and topspin the next ball. Don't think about it too much, just do it, O.K.?" And so he counts "1 . . . 2 . . . 3," And he feeds you a high push to your forehand. You're ready. You're delighted. You make the switch-over in your grip without any trouble and, just as you'd anticipated, you hit the forehand in.

Then he moves you over to your preferred forehand at the ready position in your backhand box, but makes sure, though he wants you to hit the forehand, you're at the backhand ready with your backhand grip—because before you make the switch-over you're again going to be pushing (or blocking—the idea is the same) with your backhand. "1 . . . 2 . . . 3," says your coach—and here comes one high to the center line. A fast one-step over (left foot, right foot) and you hit it in. Terrific!

Forehand Push

After you continue practicing for a while (pushing, blocking, pushing)

65

U.S. Team Member Alice Green Sonne improvising a delicately placed half block-half push shot up her opponent's backhand line. (Photo by Harry Kitselman)

with an eye to selecting and suddenly hitting the shot in (and, if necessary, hitting it in again and again and again now while you've got the table control you've been looking for), your opponent suddenly pulls another fast one. (Will it ever be so, you wonder?) Push, push, push—and then he pushes one in very close to the net on your forehand side. Of course it's in too close—and since you obviously can't stroke through the table, what do you do?

1971 World Champion Stellan Bengtsson showing the perfect racket angle for a lefty's forehand push. (Photo by Mike Hoffland)

Well, to begin with, take some consolation in the fact that this is a somewhat dangerous shot. Your opponent won't do it as often in today's game as he used to—only when you least expect him to or for other strategic reasons—because if the ball goes too deep he's setting up your forehand. Assuming, though, that you're at the backhand ready position and your opponent pushes the ball short and to your right, and that, balancing hand up, you can handle the requisite footwork, you bring the face of the racket over like a plate, so that handle and blade are parallel with the net—and then, cocking the wrist, bring the blade up into a slant (not so far as a lollipop chop position). Then, as you come forward and slightly downward, the wrist straightens out (but doesn't snap) as you, coming through, try to hold the ball on the plate of the racket as long as you can right on through and over the net.

The pushing, blocking, hitting, try-to-get-control game continues. But now your friend is not being too cooperative. He keeps "jamming" you, keeps putting the ball to your backhand, even the looked-for high one, and for a time you're exasperated. But finally it occurs to

67

Left-handed Danny Seemiller, U.S. number 1, way around on his back-hand side of the table, ready with a golfer's intent to wrist-snap a point-winning forehand in straight down the diagonal. (Photo by Mike Hoffland)

you that, just as though you've made your own middle with your backhand-at-the-ready stance, so now too must you center yourself, even at this extreme angle, to hit in your forehand.

So, remembering how earlier you'd taken that series of backward steps the length of the table, you suddenly do a little (left foot, right foot) one-step, or, better, a two-step, and—oh, oh! your timing isn't quite right. The ball is too low—but you try to topspin it in anyway and it hits the net and goes over for you. Your friendly opponent approves. He sees what you've imaginatively discovered, what he hasn't had to tell you, and knows that you really want to learn the game because you're not out there mechanically, passively, just going through the prescribed motions. Now "1 . . . 2 . . . 3" and you're already around the side of the table ready to topspin the ball into your coach's backhand corner—or, with practice, anywhere on the table.

Of course you understand (you thought you'd understood before) how really important it is to move your feet in anticipating the shot you want to hit in. Naturally, not all shots offer you the same opportunity—but with patience you'll get your chance. Of course as you and your opponent begin to play better you'll have to speed things up, more aggressively block or push to make him give you that loose (and now it won't be such a high) ball—while at the same time you'll have to keep your opponent, your counterpart, from working a loose ball out of you. For clearly if either of you can detect a conscious or unconscious 1-2-3 or whatever pattern in the other, you can take advantage of it. So, in looking to beat the opponent who most resembles you, keep on your toes, huh?

Dennis Barish, 1974 U.S. Boys Under-15 Champion, has to do some fancy footwork if he's to return ball (see throat of spectator in center of picture) by Israel's Drop Polak, 1975 U.S. Open Under-17 Champion. (Photo by Don Gunn)

chapter four

I'd like you to continue with the illusion that there's someone at the table opposite you. For in your imagination, at least, he's obviously helped you so far, else you wouldn't be this far into the book. And now with these semi-advanced loop and chop shots coming up, you'll need more of anyone's patience and encouragement.

THE LOOP

The loop is a relatively new stroke in the sport (flourished from 1960—) that was made possible by the technological advance of the sponge rubber racket—particularly the inverted pips-in kind. Contrary to what many players think, the loop may be made with the pips-out

basic strokes II

racket that both Denis Neale, the English Champion, and I use. Indeed, the loop was supposedly first demonstrated for the table tennis
world in Bombay in the 1950s by an Indian named Vyas who was
using a pips-out racket. Today, however, spinners everywhere, because of the increased spin capabilities of the inverted racket, use pips
in, at least on their forehands. So, if you really want to hop the ball,
you know which bat to use. What you give up in control, you make up
for in increased topspin potential.

Let's go back now to your original blocking position over the center
line and have that experienced player opposite you topspin while you
block. Naturally as he varies the speed of his topspin you have to cor-
respondingly vary the angle of your racket—close it, tilt it toward the
net, as the speed increases and you want to lower the trajectory of your

71

return. Yes, that's fine. You and your partner already have an exhibition steadiness—you could fool a lot of people.

Slow Loop

Suddenly, though, your opponent twirls his bat—and a strange thing happens. It's like you're facing a new player. He's changed his topspin stroke, no longer has this familiar U you're used to. Instead of casually leaning in over the table as you'd expect him to and whipping the shot through, he lets the ball drop back about a foot behind his end line. Then, bringing the racket straight up from his knees, he seems to just graze the back of the ball.

You can see, as it's spinning toward you, that it's not a hard-hit shot—that it is, in fact, a little higher than the topspin you've been accustomed to. So although you recognize a new stroke, you also see in the below-the-table upswing and the topspin coming at you similarities with the old. Anyway, you try to time the shot correctly as usual and block it back. Only—wow!—what happens? The ball goes off the table!

Your youthful-looking opponent (call him, if you like, my son Scott, who, though he's just turned 14, is an 8-year tournament veteran), goes quickly to retrieve it, comes back to the table and gives you another topspin serve down the center line. You block it back as usual and then he takes that swing straight up from below the table again. The head of the racket, you may instinctively notice, is not downward but parallel to the net, and now the ball seems to be . . . whiffed! What's going on here? How can an experienced player actually miss a ball completely that's right to him? What's he trying to do?

It isn't long before you understand that this is a "slow" loop and are into trying the shot yourself. But not, as your coach has to remind you, with your pips-out side. The idea is to allow your opponent's fairly deep block to come out and drop where you will meet it with a sharp upswing that will just slightly rub the back of the ball and send it with a relatively slow speed—but with a much greater amount of topspin than you've been used to—back to your opponent—who now, if he does return it, will block it back high and allow you to smack in a point-winning follow-up shot. Of course, as even your experienced partner's whiff will tell you, this is a delicate shot, which will demand of you much practice.

New shot or old, though, this slow loop can be handled defensively up close in two ways. First, you've seen what happens when you block normally—the ball goes off the table. If you try pushing your return, it's worse, much worse. If you step back and float the ball, it still goes much too high. How then to handle this shot? You could chop it, but since nobody has taught you how to do that yet, you'll have to find another way.

Go back to your pips-out basic block, but this time really close your racket, tilt it as if you were half going to smother the shot. Be sure you get over the ball—if necessary, by standing on your tiptoes. Your degree of success against this slow, close-to-the table spin will depend on practice and the trial and error of perfecting a light touch. Remember, try to keep the ball down, and, if possible, position it short and to your opponent's backhand to make it harder for him to loop again. I know this may not be easy, though. In 1965, Max Marinko, a former world class blocker and nine times the Champion of Canada ("You do not know who I am?" I once heard him say to someone. "You have never heard of me?"), and an unorthodox penholder with the largest racket I ever saw, lost his Canadian title to a then new breed of player whose slow, high topspin shots he just didn't know what to do with.

The other way to handle the slow loop is to step in and hit it. There's little speed on the ball and you have more time than usual to position yourself for a forehand. But since this slow loop obviously has an excessive amount of overspin, you've got to adjust your bowstring line of sight downward, to the very bottom of the net, and then let fly your U of a shot.

Of course table tennis isn't archery and you don't have a stationary target. So some risk is involved. Also, everybody's loop is different. And whereas invariably your ball will go in against a player whose game you know well, against another player you'll have trouble. Still, with practice, practice, practice, more balls will surely go in against anybody than not. And even those that don't go in will make the slow looper, who himself is trying to work free a high ball to kill, think twice about sending up even the spinniest of shots that you might zing in.

More likely, against your block or floater (and later your chop), he is not going to be swinging straight up but will modify that stroke (up and forward) by leaning both his coiled body and closed racket table-wards for speed and power. By the time we get to the chapter on advanced play he will be whirling like a discus thrower into the ball.

It's important therefore for you to learn right away how to block not just slow loops but any kind, and how to keep the ball short, just over the net, so that your opponent can't get in there to pivot his body around and so generate all that spin. Remember, if you block or float (or chop) the ball deep, he's got more and more time, more and more room, even as the ball's dropping, to spin out hard at you. Of course it works both ways—if you're giving him a judicious mixture of a floater, a chop, a (no-spin) "nothing" ball, *and topspin,* he has to adjust to the spin or no spin, else wind up and put the ball into the net or off the table. Only practice to get your timing or touch—and then more practice adapting to each different opponent at the table—will make you a winner.

Loop Drive

The slow loop is good for a change of pace, but much more effective is a faster, still close-to-the-table loop with a lower trajectory. This is as common a stroke today against any not very severely angled block or any kind of light or heavy chop as the old whip topspin was in the 1940s. The idea behind this super topspin shot is not to score a point outright, as some mistakenly think, but to force your opponent either (1) to keep returning the ball much higher than he wants to, so you can just keep spinning harder and harder until he has to miss, or (2) to allow you, when you're ready, to drive the ball or, if possible, hit it even harder, smash it, in a clear effort to win the point.

To prepare you for this loop stroke, your partner positions you at your usual backhand diamond-point edge, forehand at the ready. You're in a crouch, your knees are bent, and (though later, as you get used to the shot, you may want to play further back) you're now about two feet from the table. For this pips-in spin shot, though, your right foot is turned sideways, parallel with the end line of the table. You want to be able to lean back on this foot as you bring your left shoulder and free left arm in almost a half circle around; then, as, snapping your

At the 1973 Sarajevo World Championships: Dal Joon Lee, six-time U.S. Champion, spinning the ball against the French Champion, Jacques Secretin. (Photo by Mal Anderson)

wrist, you come through, your weight shifts back onto your left foot. Your follow-through brings the racket feather-high to your head.

You begin this loop drive about knee-high from under the table and try to time it so you'll catch the ball about bellybutton-high. About 50 percent of your swing is taken before you actually hit the ball, 50 percent after. The blade of the racket is closed and, as you swing upward and forward, you rapidly accelerate the blade, whip it, to make contact with the outside part of the ball.

Naturally you must recognize the kind of spin that's coming at you. (Perhaps in the beginning if you put some clearly defined mark on the ball you would be better able to see the way it turns in flight?) Then you must gauge the power that's necessary to counteract that spin. The angle of your racket is thus very important. Against a heavy chop, for

75

European Champ Ann-Christin Hellman of Sweden demonstrating her up-at-the-table, more-spin-than-speed forehand loop. (Photo by Mike Hoffland)

example, your racket early in your stroke might look like a held-up, overturned plate. But then, on your way to snapping your wrist as you make squared-off contact, you bring your blade up and over the ball.

The difficulty inherent in the stroke is the rub. You don't want to hit the ball as hard as you can, you want to rub it, not abrasively but hard enough and with wrist enough to send it, like an old tire, out and spinning. Perhaps it might be helpful if I allow my imagination to use a far-out image—especially to suggest the necessary power you must paradoxically try to get into this shot. Imagine that the little white ball were the planet Saturn and you a giant player in the darkness of space. If you wanted to swing out upward and forward, ideally you would rub, snap your wrist at, not Saturn but the rings that are a part of it. Wow! Wouldn't you then, with that kind of compression, send that ball spinning right out of its accustomed orbit?

Great players differ in applying varying degrees of force—

1974 U.S. Open
Under-17
Champion
Roger Sverdlik
showing his
about-as-much-
speed-as-spin
loop. (Photo by
Mike Hoffland)

Yugoslavia's great star Dragutin Surbek preparing to come into the ball at the start of his loop drive. (Photo by Mike Hoffland)

ever-changing percentages of spin and speed—to their loop drives. Generally, since the ordinary spinny loop is easy for an expert to block, speed is more important. Many times (as we'll be able to understand better from the Advanced Play chapter) the whirl-around motion is so strong, the blade is moving so fast, and the player is giving off such a wrist-snap sense of power that, in the analogy I just used, not only the rings of Saturn but Saturn itself feels the direct force of the player's racket. When that happens, the ball is really being smacked—deep through the rubber surface into the wood of the racket preparatory to being sent out all aspin again with space-hurtling speed.

The loop is thus a devastating shot against a chop or a temporizing slow low push (the kind, it used to be, that, if neither player wanted to make an aggressive move toward winning a point, could allow the game to go on theoretically for days). No wonder then that more and more players in recent years are getting away from pushing and are using instead a hopping topspin. On the offense or on the defense (and sometimes it's hard to tell which is which), both players are back from the

Surbek a moment after accelerated point of contact. (Photo by Mal Anderson)

table more and so continue historically to change the face of the game.

The style of play that was prevalent in yesterday's arena pitted the at-the-table attacker against the 20-feet-back-from-the-table defender. But today there's a fast, often in-close mixing it up between two aggressive-minded players, neither one of whom wants to retreat from the table unless the other does. Each is looking to take the initiative to open the point because statistically he knows that the one who opens the point most often wins it—and, it follows, the game and the match.

So too now, with the advent of the loop, is there much less positional pushing by average to good players—though the experts still have their spinning, sliding, javelin thrusts that go deep. Taking the place of the push is the counter-loop or at least the exchange of top-spin. And taking the place of the chop, or so some think, is the 20-foot-high lob that is so impossible to loop when it trampoline-lands and hops.

THE CHOP

Up till now, I've been talking mostly about close-to-the-table play—but without any discussion of the chop. Most table tennis uninitiates dream of retrievers as they were back 30 years ago returning shot after shot with their vicious underspin. But while this still happens, especially with Japanese choppers, it doesn't happen in the 1970s nearly as much as in decades gone by.

True, the best women players in the world—Chinese, Japanese, Korean—are choppers. (Why don't they hit the ball more? Is it because in the past in the Orient the women haven't been taught or allowed to be aggressive?) But nine out of every ten great men players are attackers—and even the Japanese choppers are always alert to any possibility where they can drive a ball or come racing in to pick-hit a shot through for a winner.

The truth is that the spin technology of the '70s makes it practically impossible for a defender to remain back from the table for long. The severe spin is just too much for him. In Calcutta, I saw what the 1975 World Runner-up Finalist Anton Stipancic of Yugoslavia, playing at his confident best, did with a turn of his wrist and an inverted racket to the former Japanese Champion Norio Takashima, probably the best chopper in the world.

It was a beautiful match to watch—it always is when a fluid hitter or spinner plays against an equally fluid defender. But after the last point was over, few spectators, though they would like to watch the graceful Takashima forever, wanted to play like him. They just didn't think, marvelous as he was, that he had the most winning style. Of course all table tennis buffs know that this opinion was not true in the past, when such defensive stars as Leach and Bergmann were more than once world champions. But it is true today. And even the best defensive player in the United States, Fuarnado Roberts, a former many-time Jamaican Champion, has recently changed his style and is now not just a pick-hitter but often an outright attacker.

Still, for 50 years, the chop has been an important part of the sport, and even for those who don't use it much it's a valuable addition when, no matter how close or how far you are from the table, you need to mix up your spin and so possibly create for yourself a point-winning opening. Understandably the chop has always been a counterstroke to topspin and in the hands of a few experts it still often is—that same Takashima, who literally scoops up balls from the floor, but who I don't think people want to pattern their games after, reached the semifinals of the 1975 World's.

Your playing partner now asks you to go to your blocker's backhand at-the-ready position—but then to take a couple of steps backward so that you're about 2½ feet behind the table. When he asks you to push the ball with him, using the pips-in side of your racket, you have to take a step in closer to the table. Later he asks you to float a couple and you have to step back about four feet. At which point he says you're ready to try something new.

He asks you to bring the racket farther back than before, about lollipop-high and, it may be, above your shoulder (there's room for variation here, depending on how hard you want to chop, how close to the table you are, how well-positioned, and what individual variations you have in your swing). Then you must bring the blade down forcefully so that it will "cut" the bottom half of the ball. The thinner the slice, the more underspin you'll get. Be sure, though, you don't jerk the stroke or stop your follow-through.

Norio Takashima's backhand chop technique.
(Photo sequence by Chui Fan Liu)

Takashima squatting and scooping the ball. (Photo by Ray Chen)

Naturally you have to begin by positioning yourself correctly. As the ball is dropping down and left to your midsection, you crouch and lean to meet it. If the ball is coming in front of you so you'll have to reach for it, it seems natural and comfortable to put your right foot forward and let it take the weight of your body. It also seems to help if I ask you to imagine that you're left-handed and that, right shoulder down, you're digging in that garden you might one day have if you'd spend your free time cultivating it. If the ball is not going to drop in front of you (so much depends on your anticipation, your timing, your footwork), it's best to extend your left foot to the side and perhaps a little back. What you do *not* want to do is cross your right foot in front of the left one. Also, as soon as you stroke the ball through, center yourself in the ready position again.

You're finding this chop-down stroke harder to learn than the floater. It has something to do with the wrist and the swivel of the more upright lollipop face of the racket as you come into the ball. You're

84

used to just kind of easin' through. You instinctively don't think you're going to become a good chopper.

After some encouragement, though, you think you begin to feel a little backspin tug on the ball. And when your opponent deliberately lets a shot or two go by him and you see the ball fall to the floor, bounce a little forward and sideways and start to "die," you're very pleased with your power over the ball—all the different spins you already can make it do. True, you're better at some shots than others, but you're not complaining. Might as well try here in the beginning to see what it would be like to be an all-around player. You're forming some judgments about what's best for you, though. You're a doer—and that means you can't think too much. You learn by doing.

Drop Shot

Just when you think you're getting tired of practicing the chop, your opponent suddenly slips another little surprise at you. He "masks" a topspin shot, comes in over the ball, arm upraised, but then doesn't follow through hard, just drops the ball over the net. You're immediately rejuvenated. You want to try it—it looks like something you can do. Looks just like an in-close push shot.

And as you soon find out, it is. Except that you've got to contact the ball at the top of the bounce. You must also be very delicate in your touch, so that the ball will go "dead," will bounce several times on your opponent's side of the table. For a while, you and your partner practice varying the pace on your topspins and returns. Now that you're looking for the drop shot when you're back from the table, it's not so easy to catch you on it—or so you think. You also learn through trial and error that you should not try to drop a ball that comes deep.

As you're taking your turn topspinning, you begin to realize that when your partner chops the ball, really chops it, you have to lift your pips-in forehand more than you did your pips-out one. Your partner's no robot. He agrees—says you've made a good observation. Urges you to crouch a little more, roll the whole left side of your body more as you step back on that right leg, then come upward and forward, snapping the wrist, rubbing the ball through. He's more experienced than he looks. What he knows but you don't yet is that everything

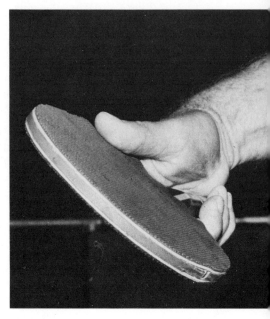

Triptych showing the way a blocker must angle his racket depending on the severity of the topspin that's coming at him.

you're doing is like in the way of experimentation. Is like slow motion. As the lessons go on, everything will speed up.

When your opponent loads his chop, though, you'd like to send that Saturn-ball spinning away from him and out of his court. Of course—though how can you know it?—that's exactly what Itoh was trying to do against Germany's now retired Eberhard Scholer, perhaps the greatest of modern defenders in the 1969 World Championship final in Munich. Until down two games to none, he wised up and just started spinning to set up his next shot, and the next, and the next, to eventually win the match. Now if any student reading this book could have seen that!

Your friendly but serious-minded opponent ·asks you to chop close-in on your forehand side, using the same cut stroke and stance (in reverse) that you used for the backhand chop. For some reason, you prefer chopping with your backhand. It's more karate-like and aesthetically pleasing to you. "That's just as well," says your young-looking instructor (who's also formed his own opinions). "There are better uses for the forehand."

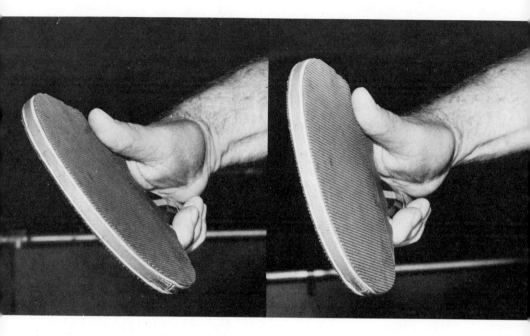

And he proceeds to demonstrate. Has you stay at the table while he goes several feet back. Then asks you to push some balls deep to his forehand. You do and he lets them drop practically out of sight before suddenly, as if his closed stroke came up from his shoelaces, he and the ball come leaping at you. You forget for a moment, and instead of blocking the ball you push it. It goes way off the table. The next time, though, you're ready for it. You close your racket and—somehow its sidespin gets by you. Again it comes and again you close your racket, but the great amount of overspin still takes it off the table. You tilt your racket in still more, determined to watch the ball even as it makes contact with your bat. Your return hits the back edge. You just got in a winner.

Now, after some more blocking practice, your partner delays getting back to the chop, though that's the lesson for today, because he sees you're really not too interested in it. So he suggests something a little different. "Forehand to forehand," he calls it—and you both topspin to each other, easy at first, close to the table, then moving back, then back farther, each starting to hop the ball. What you need for all this is steadiness, however, and at this point you don't have it. Still, the changing pace, the need for just the right timing, appeals to you. You wonder how many more playing combinations and mirror patterns there are. You'd guess a lot.

O.K., time to go back to the chop. You can obviously return the simple topspins much better than even the moderate loop drive. You try to load up your chop but it still comes out pretty much like a floater. The ball always seems to come too fast, you can't dig in very well, you don't follow through as you should, and too often the ball goes off the table. You understand well enough how the loop was devised to counteract the chop, but you don't understand how anybody can ever chop hard enough to get the ball down.

Your coach is sympathetic, knows what you're thinking, understands more than you do your problem. Although he believes only practice can really help you, he asks me to take over, say anything I want in closing this chapter. I try one last time to be as technical as I can.

To execute the backhand chop, you're in a squared-off, shoulder-length stance, centered maybe 6 feet behind your backhand box. Your body's leaning in, and you're ready to put your weight on the ball of either foot should the shot demand it. Some choppers have an exercise where, to keep from being heavy on their feet, they stand on tiptoe, moving the heel up and down about as many times as they also do push-ups.

As the ball comes topspinning slightly to your left, you're careful not to hurry your backswing, careful not to bring it back faster than the oncoming ball. You take the racket up and back anywhere from heart-high to over the shoulder, then, extending your left arm out for balance, you bring the racket sharply down and, as it rubs against the lower part of the ball, smoothly forward and through—in a nearly straight line or a right-to-left sidespin-backspin movement, finishing with both arms out, birdlike.

If you're chopping up closer to the table and can sidespin the ball into your opponent's forehand when he expects it (as usual) to his backhand, you might even be able to catch him off guard and give yourself a chance to pick-hit.

Some at-the-ready choppers have the racket squared off, others hold it flat, plate-like. Some, on seeing the ball coming toward them, bring

In Sook Na, U.S. number 1 Women's player, showing backhand chop.
(Photo by Mal Anderson)

the bat higher up, even into a lollipop position or beyond, then come
down sharply, sinking their knees, varying their spin, actual or faked.

If the ball comes topspinning to your left side, the left leg is
stretched over, foot pointing to the side, while the right foot rolls right
but remains secured by the big toe, which, after you follow through,
will allow your weight to spring lightly back into the ready position or,
since you're always moving, always taking tiny steps, a nearly identical ready position.

89

South Korea's Chung Hyun Sook, 1975 U.S. Open Champ, about to make a forehand chop return. (Photo by Mal Anderson)

If you're chopping on the forehand, your left foot may be lined up almost parallel to the center line, but your right foot will face sideways. As, knees slightly bent, you're about to sink down into the chop, your body weight shifts over to the right and you come slicing sharply down around and through, chopping the middle of the ball as it drops in front of your right kneecap, and then shifting your weight back to your left foot.

Footwork, of course, is even more important for a chopper than a looper, and unless it's absolutely necessary (you do always want to get the ball back, come what may), any crossing of the feet is to be a-voided. Sometimes it's possible for a very good chopper to still look awkward. One coach I know, on seeing a Chinese woman player, a recent World Finalist, said, "If she'd have come, an unknown, to my club, I would have told her to go out and run for two months and then come back."

Sophisticated defenders, men or women, generally use "slow" rubber so that the ball will stay on their rackets longer and they'll have more control. They also often vary their stroke, take the ball higher, lower, sometimes more to the front, other times to the back, and often

Chung Hyun Sook about to swing her racket head down into a forehand chop return of Ann-Christin Hellman's drive. (Photo by Mal Anderson)

vary the angle of their blade as well as the amount of wrist they use on each chop, the better to try and fool their opponents.

The new anti-topspin rubber can often be used to great advantage. Against a loop, the antispin ball seems to float back, though with the suggestion of heaviness—seems, unpredictably, to be shaky or wobbly. Against a push or chop it often comes back with topspin—which the looper, if he's not careful, may misread.

As the years go by, the defensive players are thus learning more and more—and yet they're winning less and less. However, though I personally am not much of a chopper, I still remember that one day back when I was 10 years old and opened the pages of *Life* to see Lou Pagliaro, then the U.S. Champion and a chopper. One picture showed a close-up of the sole of one of his sneakers, on which of course he'd been continually pivoting. This sole had to be replaced because it had a big hole in it.

That picture, over which I marveled, perhaps more so than over anything I've ever seen in a sports page since, went deep within me.

chapter five

Each player has his own special serves, often slightly different from anyone else's. So, regardless of what you read, don't let yourself be fooled—only through the trial and error of competitive play can you get used to them.

I remember seeing China's Liang Ko-liang for the first time in the 1971 Nagoya World Championships. He was using a racket with two different kinds of sponge—one for his forehand and one for his back-hand side. At first this was surprising to me, but—just as his success has since resulted in any number of imitators using inverted on one side and anti-topspin or pips-out on the other—I soon saw the point of it.

Liang had his peculiar habit of crouching low and twirling his bat under the table before he served. Why? Because with those two differ-ent sheets of rubber, each same-colored side of his racket provided

service and receive

him, as he unrelentingly rose to the attack, with two very changeable kinds of spin—and he didn't want his opponent, who might be watching his racket, to see which side was which.

Indeed, Liang's confused opponent couldn't even hear which side was which because every time Liang served, at the precise moment he made contact with the ball, he stamped his foot loudly. The effect of which—like a lion's roar before the spring—had to startle, then half paralyze, the man not nerved to it.

You, though, reading this book, are beginning to get used to some things. You've already seen that the spin technology of the sponge racket has changed the sport dramatically in recent years, so much so that attacking players now far outnumber defensive ones. As percentage charts in European or Asian table tennis magazines show, the first

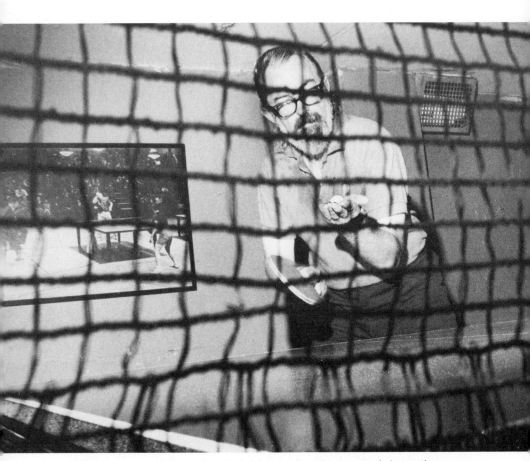

Many a server hopes to catch his receiver in a net of deception.

spinner or hitter who can quickly, aggressively, gain control of the ball figures to win the point—and win it fast. Naturally, given this new situation where both players are fighting for the immediate advantage, the serve and serve return have become much more important than they were in the '40s or '50s, the long rally, attack-and-retrieve days of the hard rubber bat.

Of course, as the history of table tennis shows, early tournament players way back in the '30s were looking for a quick service advantage. Some had taken to finger-spinning serves into or against their rackets—and herein obviously, after many a bewildered opponent had protested, was the rub. Often even a champion could not read the quirky bounces the ball might take. Finally the International Table Tennis Federation had to establish rules for a "legal" serve, one that would not unduly favor the server or threaten to change a serious tournament match into a whacky Buster Keaton comedy.

Today the service law is quite clear, and anyone who expects to play in tournament competition must know it—else risk being faulted. The ball has to be held above table level and so be visible to the umpire at all times; it must be thrown up as vertically as possible from the palm of the hand (the fingers cannot be cupped but must be outstretched together, with the thumb free); and, as it drops, the ball has to be hit from behind the server's end line.

Restrictive or uncomfortable as all this may sound, it becomes second nature to any serious player and he soon learns how to impart legally all kinds of seemingly mysterious hops and stops to the ball.

To take one outstanding example (and on my well-known "Ping-Pong diplomacy" trip I played a friendly match against a fellow in Shanghai who served like this), Hsu Shao-fa, the so-called "miracle server," a member of the winning Chinese team at the recent World Championships in India, sometimes throws the ball six feet high on his serve.

As with increasing speed the ball falls, Hsu watches it carefully (like a magician his illusion) and then twists his waist, pivots into the ball with such a fast deceptive motion that his spin-imparting racket head might be coming up (which means one kind of spin) or coming down (which means another). Although Shao-fa's head is not immediately moving to watch his follow-through (any more than a golfer's would be), the ball is off and hopping—as unpredictable in its bounce or no bounce as a Mexican jumping bean.

From my experience, then, I know there is no easy way for you to be taught the year-by-year secrets of the best servers in the world. Moreover, even if these players could be persuaded to part with their bread and butter knowledge gained from years of hard work, you would first have to be a very good student of the game to put what they would tell you to use. So, for you and me, in this book, one thing at a time.

The forehand and backhand serves I'm about to describe for you are ones—involving 20 or so variations in spin and placement—I've built

95

LEGAL AND ILLEGAL SERVES

(Photos by Mal Anderson)

Legal—hand is held
flat, thumb free

Illegal—hand is cupped

Legal—ball is thrown up

Illegal—ball is below playing surface

Legal—ball can be outside the side
line if it's also behind the end line

Illegal—ball can't be contacted
in front of end line

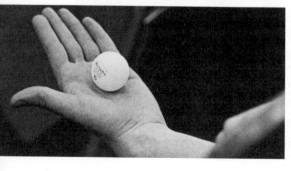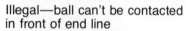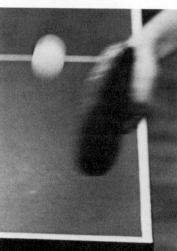

Ingemar Wikstrom of Sweden waiting to receive the impossible-to-practice-in-your-basement service of China's Li Ching-kuang. Wikstrom of course must not look at the ball but at what the Chinese is going to do to it when it comes down. (Photo by Mal Anderson)

up over the years in my own tournament repertoire. And, given each player's trial by combat variation of them, they are basic to all good players, even to world champions. So if to begin with you've incentive enough to try to master these, you may be on your way to playing in international competition yourself.

FOREHAND SERVES FROM BACKHAND SIDE OF TABLE

I use mostly forehand serves from the far left side—my backhand side—of the table. I do this because whenever I can I play with my pips-out (not flat, not inverted) racket a serve-and-one attacking game, am always willing to hit (rather than spin) the third ball. In other

97

words, after (1) my serve and (2) my opponent's return, I want to (3) win the point outright if I can with a smash. If I can't, if my opponent returns my serve too well, I quickly try to set up a fifth-ball attack. That is, I try to maneuver my service follow-up to a spot on the table where (4) my opponent's second return will let me (5) smash in a winner. Therefore I always want my body position, my hand position, to be ready to further my forehand attack.

To serve forehands I adopt a basic stance. First I center myself a foot and a half behind the left diamond-point edge of the table. Extend an imaginary line out from this pointed edge and it would hit at a juncture of my upper thigh and crotch. Then drop a line down and it would hit my left instep. The position of my feet and the imaginary lines suggest an "open" stance, as in golf.

My knees are bent, I'm in a semi-crouch, and most of my weight is on the balls of my feet—more on the right foot than on the left—while my left heel is actually off the ground. I'm leaning forward, ready in my follow-up to extend my free hand up and out for balance as I transfer my weight to the ball of my left foot and do a very short, very fast fencer's two-step (left foot, right foot; left foot, right foot) sideways. This will get me into the proper attacking position for the anticipated return to my backhand or middle—for certainly my opponent will try his best not to make it easy for me to hit my strong forehand, will invariably not put his return into the open part of the table.

Obviously much of my effectiveness will depend upon the strength of my legs and my willingness to move fast to take the offense. Peculiarly I hold the ball higher than almost any other player—heart-high just behind the table edge—and throw it only a couple of inches up. As it immediately descends, and I watch it, I must decide, even as in the background I may see my opponent move, if I'm at the last second going to put it precisely where I'd planned to.

Often before I serve I unconsciously bounce the ball on the racket or, with either my free hand or the racket head, bounce the ball to the floor—the better, I think, in this age of everything's-got-to-be-quick-quick-quick, to concentrate. Technically speaking, too much of this ball-bouncing is severely frowned on, but in 17 years of tournament competition I have never seen anyone faulted for doing it—not even at World Championships where the rules are often more strictly

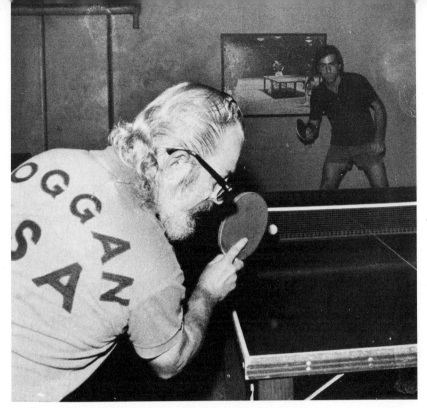

A deceptive "no-look" down-the-line topspin serve.

enforced than they are elsewhere. At least I've never been accused of trying to fast-serve an opponent who wasn't ready.

Fast Topspin Serves Deep

To serve fast topspin serves deep anywhere on the table, I begin by holding the racket parallel to my extended service hand, with the center of the racket face in an imaginary line with the ball. My racket is closed; the tip of it is in a direct line with the right net post.

To serve fast down my left sideline, to bring the racket head through and over the ball, is thus very easy—so easy that with practice I've been able to make the serve much more effective by not looking in that direction as, mixing up my serves, I suddenly zip one down there. The advantage of this down-the-line serve is not just that it occasionally catches your opponent by surprise but that it gives you the whole table in which to exploit your follow-up forehand.

You'll rarely ace anyone these days but if any serve will do it, it's this one—especially if you've consistently been serving to your opponent's backhand and he, anticipating a similar serve again, has taken to running around his backhand with his forehand.

Moreover, by breaking my wrist as I come through the ball, I don't have to serve down the line—I can push a fast serve far to the right, cross court, where it's often hard for my right-handed opponent to backhand the ball aggressively enough to stop me from quickly following up my advantage.

A fast serve to the middle—or just a little to either side of that, into the receiver's hip or wherever it's hardest for him to handle—is especially effective if you've been serving him left and right.

Whenever I'm going to serve a fast one—either straight topspin or sidespin—I make sure my thumb has dropped from its blocker's defensive position on the right side of the racket face and two of my fingers have slid down to the end of the handle. This little trick allows me to whip the racket into the ball with more speed than I would otherwise get.

Remember, though, many of your opponents will quickly get used to straight fast serves. The risk then is that, since the ball bounces deep, the ready receiver, particularly if he stands fairly well back from the table, has the time either to chop the ball effectively or—and this is more likely and much more dangerous—to counter the ball back deep at you. This would at once nullify any over-the-table advantage you, moving in towards the net, hoped to have. Keep in mind that the farther back your opponent is, the more effective a short serve would be.

Sidespin Serves Deep

To serve twisting left-to-right sidespin serves deep (which means the ball is spinning farther into your right-handed opponent's backhand), I use my basic stance and beginning address. I hold the racket parallel to my extended service hand. But this time the face of the racket is open, not closed. And now my wrist is cocked up and back and the racket is arced up over my right shoulder—to be then brought down in a sweeping left-to-right wrist-snap motion across the ball. As I finish the stroke my follow-through either curves out towards my opponent's diamond-point backhand edge or slices into his too cramped middle.

When I bring my racket through the ball, as I pivot and my weight begins to shift to my left foot, I am already preparing to move into the two-step follow-through that I hope will enable me to smack in the return. I know from experience, though, that I must be very careful not to start moving my feet until I've actually served the ball.

If you want to twist a left-to-right serve into your opponent's forehand, obviously you'll have to move over to your right to have table room to do it. This may or may not be dangerous, depending on whether your opponent can return the ball to your backhand and whether you can get over there quickly enough to maintain the forehand advantage you want.

Short Serves

To serve short chop or sidespin chop serves I use exactly the same crouching forehand stance and address I used for the fast deep serves. The idea of course is to try to keep your opponent guessing whether you're going to serve long or short; right, left, or middle. The more identical your beginning body and hand movements, the more effective your serves.

This time, though, my cocked wrist brings my open racket face no farther than shoulder-high, and I serve with much less force than I would were I serving a deep twister. Using a downward arc and keeping my racket hand in rather close to my body I cut the ball under its center. If I also want left-to-right sidespin, I chop left to right across the ball.

The whole point of serving short is to try and prevent your opponent from taking over the offense. Though you want to serve short, you don't want to serve too short, because then the receiver's course of action is clear—he must simply tap the ball back and hope you can't follow up the shot close to the net. It's better if you tempt your opponent into forcing an aggressive return or pushing the ball back high enough so you can get at it.

If the short serve is to be effective, it must (were it allowed to) bounce twice on the opponent's side of the table. If it doesn't, it's not short enough and can easily be attacked.

A no-spin or topspin serve?

To serve a short nothing ball to any part of the table, I deceptively use pretty much the same open racket motion in the beginning—but then I don't cut the shot. On the contrary, as coming through I'm about to make contact with the ball, I suddenly turn the lollipop face of the racket upward and stroke with the wrist as if waving goodbye.

To serve a short topspin serve I again, just before contact, turn up the face of the racket and forcefully brush through, getting overspin by stroking the top part of the ball.

You'll soon find it's amazing how many good players, given of course so little time to see and think at the table, just won't be able to anticipate the difference in your changing spin. They quickly look but they don't really see what you're doing with that racket head.

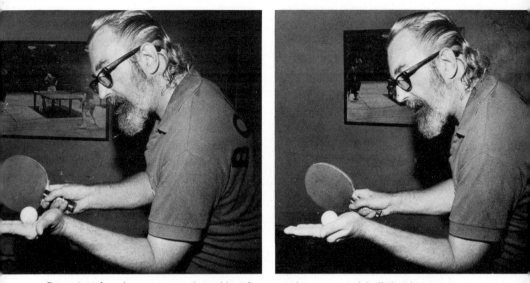

Open bat for chop serve; closed bat for topspin serve—this little change in the racket angle makes a big difference.

For instance, your opponent is likely to pop up a short serve—one into his middle particularly—which, if you're ready, you can smash away. Psychologically, the receiver sometimes hasn't got it clear in his head where he wants to return the ball and so, slightly confused, he often pushes his return higher than he should. He's just as likely, too, to think that your topspin has chop and so will return the simplest of short serves off the table. Give him every chance to go wrong by constantly mixing up your serves.

BACKHAND SERVES FROM BACKHAND SIDE OF TABLE

To serve with my backhand from the backhand side of the table, I change my basic stance and address. I.move over a little to my right (the left end line extended would hit at a juncture of my thigh and crotch) and I stand a little farther back, about two feet, from the table. I move right, not just because it will reduce the open area to be covered

103

by my forehand—which of course is not at the ready position—but also because I need more room away from that diamond-point edge to serve safely. I like to stand another half foot back of the table while serving because if I get the chance, even if the return is fairly deep, I want to follow with a backhand kill.

Short Chop Serve

I use the short chop serve sparingly (in singles, that is; it comes in very handy in doubles) and generally I put it into my opponent's right-hand box just over the net, close to the middle line. You'd be surprised how often he returns it mechanically to my backhand, little realizing I'm not in my usual ready forehand position but am waiting to backhand flick it in for the point.

To execute this serve properly, I hold the racket (head flat, like it's a plate) parallel to the end line. With my free hand I throw the ball up and, making along the way a crossbones of my wrists, I arc the racket head up towards my left shoulder, then bring it back down, cutting into and under the center of the ball and smoothly following through, as if holding the ball on the racket (back into the plate position again).

Fast Topspin Serve

To serve a fast backhand serve, I adopt my usual backhand stance but in my address I close the racket to its block position. Then, making sure my thumb is steadying the back of the blade, I sweep the racket back and through, snapping my wrist as I make contact with the ball. This serve is especially effective if it comes as a surprise—if you unexpectedly use it after you've given your opponent nothing but short chop serves to his mid-section.

The beginning positions of the rackets in these chop and topspin serves are very different from each other, but most likely the receiver will be conscious only of a vague backhand movement. If you can snap your wrist well and cover the ball, it is just as easy, by taking pretty much the same backswing, to send the serve fast and deep as it is to send it slow and short.

Even very experienced players can be deceived by experts who take

Singapore's Chris Yuen cradling a backhand can't-be-sure-how-it'll-turn-out serve. (Photo by Mal Anderson)

different racket positions that at first appear to signal different spins but don't, or positions that at first appear to signal similar spins but don't.

Sidespin Serve Deep

To serve a twisting right-to-left sidespin backhand serve deep, I take up my position to the left of the diamond-point edge. But I am not in my usual crouch because I need more leverage to come down hard on the ball and take a longer follow-through.

To begin with, my racket is in a block position. I take it pendulum-like back more than shoulder-high, then bring it down through again, as forcefully I break my wrist right to left across the ball and swing through in an arc out and upwards towards my opponent's cross-court edge. In the beginning my weight is mostly on the ball of my right foot, but my left heel is arched high and as I follow through I will shift my weight over onto my left foot in preparation for a very short, very

105

Sweden's Carl Johan Bernhardt hatching a tricky forehand serve against Jamaica's Les Haslem. (Photo by Mal Anderson)

fast three-step (left foot, right foot; left foot, right foot; left foot, right foot) follow-up, which will put me in a position to hit a forehand.

All this presumes of course that my opponent has trouble with this particular spin serve—otherwise, since it doesn't favor my forehand, I won't use it at all. Generally speaking, it's good to try out your repertoire of serves early in the match. If your opponent is really troubled by one, don't use it again unless you have to. I mean, it's always nice to know you have a little something in reserve.

FOREHAND SERVES FROM
FOREHAND SIDE OF TABLE

It's a generally accepted truth that any suddenly "different" serve, even if it involves nothing more than an exaggerated body movement, often wins you the point—and sometimes that one point is all you need to take the match. In Calcutta, at the World Championships, I saw the 1975 World Champion, Istvan Jonyer of Hungary, use a special forehand serve when the going got tough. He stood sideways just to the right of the center line, then dropped down into a squat position, leveled his eyes just above the end line, curled up his arms, and snipe-hooked a low trajectory serve that even a fellow world class player missed.

All the serves from the forehand side of the table, executed with the same varying techniques I've already described in discussing serves from the backhand side, force me to move even faster to my left than I would normally—that is, if I want to follow them with my serve and one forehand. Yet to keep my opponent from getting too familiar with my usual serves from the backhand side of the table, to keep him from "getting set," I occasionally serve from this side short chop serves, short nothing-ball serves, and lightning-fast cross-court serves. Sometimes, too, I'll vary already proven serves, will suddenly serve one very fast into the receiver's middle.

The main thing is to mix up the serves, relying heavily on those that through the course of the match work best. Remember, though, the danger in these forehand serves is that you are serving into your right-handed receiver's strong point—his point-winning forehand. Don't forget, he's a mirror image of you—he knows that to win he has to attack, too.

The patterns of your own and your opponents' serve play is something you as a serious student of the sport should chart. The more unpredictably you can play, the more difficult it will be for even the best players in your immediate tournament area to get onto your game.

BACKHAND SERVES FROM FOREHAND SIDE OF TABLE

These deep or short, fast or chop-slow serves I've been discussing I also use from the forehand side, mostly in doubles, where it's necessary for me to serve from my right-hand "box" into my opponent's right-hand "box." Your changing doubles partner may prefer you to serve to the left or right of him, depending on whether he's left- or right-handed, or whether he's more comfortable, feels he has more of the table if, in circling around back into position, you move to the left or right of him.

Also, since more than occasionally in singles play, you'll be up against a lefty (three of the five United States Men's Team members to

107

the 1975 World Championships in India were left-handed), it often pays you to be able to reverse yourself and, even at the expense of not always being able to follow with a hard forehand, serve all your best serves into your southpaw opponent's backhand.

At any event, one good way for you to try to quickly adapt to today's fast attacking play is to learn to serve to and from all parts of the table. Which means practice, practice, practice. Monotonous practice. Unless, like Danny Seemiller, the number-one American player, you continue to inventively try out a number of crazy serves—a few of which after some patient refinement suddenly do not seem crazy at all, not when they begin to win you points in tournament matches.

You can also make your service practice much more interesting by placing objects on the table to try to hit—a coin, a broken ball, even (since you've decided smoking is bad for you and you want to get rid of that last pack of Camels) a cigarette. And if you have trouble getting a partner to help you pick up all those balls, why not buy or rent a robot that, besides serving and returning the ball to you in very predictable (and, as you get better, too predictable) ways, will also, with its batting cage-like net, save you many back-breaking hours.

Anyway, keep at it. Learning how to serve well requires more mental than physical energy. With a little imagination you can always improve with age. I once lost a vital game point to a kooky middle-aged "knuckle-ball" server. At the time I thought this fellow had mis-stroked his serve because of course he'd completely missed the ball with his racket and was therefore very lucky that the ball, catching me off guard both in its direction and lack of sound, had gone on the table. Imagine my surprise when later I found out that he'd actually been practicing this legal but very peculiar serve for just such an occasion 15 minutes a day!

Nope, you're never too old to learn.

THE RETURN OF SERVE

To receive my opponent's serve, I'm a foot and a half behind the table —not so far that I can't one-step in and reach a short one. I'm closer to the end line than many players because I'm a blocker. Which means I'm using my basic squared-off stance (my left foot is just outside the side line) to cover the backhand "box" in front of me.

service and receive

Left-handed Stellan Bengtsson at his backhand ready, awaiting his opponent's serve. (Photo by Mike Hoffland)

If my opponent serves from his backhand side, I try to anticipate from his body movement and the position of his racket whether he's going to give me a ball I can hit. If he is, I'll be prepared to rapidly move out of my fairly relaxed position at the ready, extend my balancing free hand up and out, and fast two-step left. However, if I smack that ball hard and he's waiting to quickly block it back into my forehand court, I often will not be able to come out of my follow-through fast enough to get over there and even get my racket on the ball.

Some players, particularly forehand-minded penholders waiting to receive an opponent's serve somewhere on the open table, hug their backhand diamond-point edge. But to cover that much open ground that fast you not only have to be marvelously conditioned, you have to be under 30, the almost mandatory retirement age for many a world class player.

Of course I too would always like to be able to take the ball with my forehand, but I've just got to accept the fact that the server has the advantage. By serving into my backhand he forces me to receive with my backhand and so puts me on the defensive. There's no way around it. The server has control—he knows where he's going to serve the ball and I don't. If I'm there at my backhand edge hugging the forehand, my right-handed opponent zipping a cross-court serve at me forces me to fast-step far to the right. Now, even if I do hit a pretty good attacking shot on the run, he can still quickly block it back to my backhand side and any forehand advantage I might momentarily have gained I've immediately more than lost.

Normally, then, after expecting and generally getting a serve to my backhand, I will block or push it back—close my racket or open it depending on whether the spin is top or chop. Occasionally my opponent's short serve will be longer and higher than he wanted it to be and I will be able to snap-backhand it in. Long ago I made up my mind to boldly follow through with such an opportunity regardless of how close the score was. If the shot is there to hit, hit it.

One serve that's very difficult for me to return, though, is a chop serve to my forehand up short by the net. Invariably I open the face of the racket and just try to touch the ball back. Trouble is, I can't lift the ball with any force cross-court because it's so close to the net, and my opponent, realizing this, is the better prepared to position his next shot and, worse, to begin spinning the ball at me. And if he spins I'm forced either to counter, which can be reckless, or go into my block defense with my opponent already in close to the net and the spin already starting to build.

If, when I'm receiving, the server moves over and takes up his ready position on the forehand side, I, opposite him, move right too, am then squared off just left of the center line. Most important in returning serve is your ability to adjust to your opponent's varying service moves. When he moves, you'd better move, too. Table tennis, like billiards, is something of an extended board game, similar to chess in that positional advantage is so important.

Tips on Returning Service

As your opponent gets set to serve, you must consciously ask yourself important questions. Where is my opponent going to serve this ball? How does he expect me to return it? How will he follow up his serve? What can I do to position the ball so my opponent can't take his best shot and sooner or later I can? After a while, though, these questions had better be instinctive—you don't have much time out there. Better maybe you study your opponent while he's playing someone else. Combine analysis with what most players simply follow—their intuition.

If you're having trouble returning your opponent's spinny top and sidespin serves, try to catch the ball early, like a block, and, touching the ball more lightly than you might think necessary, aim for the middle of the table. Also, strange as it might sound, you might try smacking these serves, provided of course you can get in a position to do it. You just might get a couple in so your opponent will think twice, especially if the score is close, of giving you the chance to boldly hit one or two in. If you threaten to score like this when he serves his best, you gain a great deal psychologically. I mean, if you really are having trouble with certain serves and your opponent is allowed to ruthlessly follow them up, building up his confidence by controlling the game and powerfully hitting balls in, what's the point? What have you got to lose by trying to be aggressive yourself?

At any rate, any given type of service should not always be returned in the same manner, particularly if you can only just hold your own with it. When the game is close, a single unexpected return to a different part of the table might win you the point outright.

Be sure to watch the server's body movements and especially his racket. Never mind, for the moment, about the ball. (The time to watch the ball, of course, is when it's in play but also in between points to improve your concentration.) If, for example, the ball is thrown up mystifyingly high, don't let your eyes follow it. Even very good players sometimes make this mistake. I remember last year in an international match in Kingston, Les Haslem, the Jamaican champion, got fooled by the English player Ian Horsham. Horsham had been throwing the ball high and pretended to again. He crouched down, brought his body and service hand up, then dramatically looked up. And so did Haslem—just as Horsham with perfect sleight-of-hand timing quickly served the ball short. Haslem was aced—and by a serve that any beginner watching Horsham's racket would have returned.

One last piece of advice here before we move on to some discussion of strategy and then to various aspects of advanced play. As you come up against more and more players, you'll see some of them trying this Chinese "throw-up" (also called "slow-up") serve. But like the tricks of master illusionists, such secrets do not come easy to every would-be imitator. Chances are these players are just trying for a psychological advantage. Don't be intimidated. More often than not, the throw-up serve in the hands of amateurs or even fairly good players is really weak and ought to be attacked—especially by anyone serious enough about the sport to read this book. Have the guts to do it.

chapter six

"What's it take to be a good coach?" I asked Alex Ehrlich, long a celebrated table tennis aficionado and 3-time World Men's Finalist.

"Thirty years' practice in different countries," he answered, and though he was smiling we both knew it was no joke.

Because of the very fast, ever-changing way the sport is being played in the '70s, with all the varying new spins and styles, a coach is much more important now than he was 25 years ago. Today, every player —beginner or world champion—needs a coach, or at least a friend or fellow enthusiast, someone who believes in the player's potential, who can motivate him, inspire him, if need be even pamper him.

Laszlo Bellak, the great international player who, in his mid-sixties is still winning trophies, was once heard by his roommate, another great Hungarian player, Sandor Glancz, talking in his sleep. "Captain," Bel-

strategy—
with or without a coach

lak was saying, "who is the greatest player you ever had on your team?"
There was a pause and then Bellak said. "Thank you, Captain."

Above all, the player—especially a player with deep, deep desire,
like Bellak—must be convinced that the coach (who often is or has
been a good player himself) knows more than he, the player, knows.
The best coaches not only can improve your play after a match—by
examining the notes they've taken while you were playing or seeing
your games replayed on film—but, much more importantly, can give
you an almost instant analysis even as you're out there at the table
against an opponent. Naturally this often makes the difference between
winning and losing.

It's very important, too, that a player not be subjected to well-
intentioned advice by those friends of his watching the match. Let

Unexpected strategy. (Photo by Mal Anderson)

them, if they really want to help, talk to the player's coach—if their advice is sound, the coach will know it and pass it on. Otherwise, the advice the player gets might even be conflicting and will only confuse him—that is, if he allows himself to pay any attention to it.

I myself have never wanted advice, never asked for it, never taken it from anybody *while I was playing*. And rarely when I've played a tough match have I ever, for any reason, looked at anyone in the

If you can't get to the ball one way, try another. Two great world doubles champions, Laszlo Bellak of Miami and Sol Schiff of New York, putting on an exhibition at the start of the 1974 U.S. Open in the Oklahoma City Myriad. (Photo by Mal Anderson)

Fuarnado Roberts of the U.S. Team in one of the 1972 China-U.S.A. matches played in this country. Note Chinese photographer taking pictures of Roberts' unseen Chinese opponent.

audience. And while I'm sure I've lost matches that a look or two at a coach might well have won for me, I also think my dependence solely on self has increased my strength of concentration, my will, at the table, and so has allowed me to defeat more opponents than I would have even with outside help.

FILM YOUR PLAY

Much of the success of the Chinese in world table tennis has come about because they have so many coaches for their players. Tournament after tournament they are always pooling information about how their competition plays and then collectively digesting this material, especially by using movie after movie (the Chinese film more matches than anyone

115

else in the world). Then, through group discussion, they plan their players' strategies so that they can exploit their opponents' weaknesses.

The first time I realized how in-the-know the Chinese were was the first time I saw them—on their reappearance at the World Championships in Nagoya, Japan in 1971 after a 6-year absence brought on by their Cultural Revolution. On the last day of practice in the Aichi Stadium before the tournament matches were to begin, they had entered silently, some sixty strong in uniform maroon jump suits or official grey button-down suits, and had tafen a block of seats in the empty balcony upstairs, and were now watching, like people in a hovering spaceship, a particular player in a court adjacent to me below. Who was that player? Eighteen-year-old Stellan Bengtsson of Sweden, seeded number 10 in the tournament, who, as it turned out, by playing superbly, was to win the World Singles Championship.

So they already knew, even as they reappeared so mysteriously on the scene, which player most warranted all their collective attention—though in this case there was nothing finally they could do about his victory.

The Japanese also put a great deal of emphasis on strategic camera work, on getting sequence shots of their best players. At any tournament the world over, Ogimura, the famous Japanese player and coach, might be seen pushing a button on his camera right after he's told one of his players on the court something. A good visual aid, huh? Had this player made the adjustment Ogimura asked him to make? If he hadn't, could he later look at the film and still imagine he had? And if he did make the adjustment, how had his opponent reacted? Did the coach really know what he was talking about? It was all there in the mirror of history—irrefutable, wasn't it?

Maybe then it wouldn't be such a bad idea, if you're really serious about your game, to have someone take, say, a 50-foot reel of you playing? What you actually do out there on the court might differ considerably from your ideal play. And you might pick up some invaluable pointers that, human nature being what it is, if you didn't see, you wouldn't believe.

SERVICE AND RECEIVE STRATEGY

The first thing a good coach does is watch you play. He judges your

116

strengths and weaknesses—sees what strokes come to you naturally. If it's clear a player doesn't want to be a chopper, there's no reason he has to be. It's not necessary for anyone to be an all-around player. Surbek, for example (his overdeveloped right arm makes his normal left one look as though it's been stricken with infantile paralysis), is a great world-class competitor, but if you took his all-important forehand away from him there'd be 100 players in the United States who could beat him. Granted, however, that it's theoretically possible for someone to be a world champion with a game strategically built around one unstoppable smash shot, he still has to get himself into position to hit that shot—and so fully 50 percent of the student's practice time ought to be taken up with service and receive.

To be a good table tennis player you have to be able to read the server's spin. (Imagine the frustrated golfer who can't read the roll of the greens and so can never put the ball where he wants to.) But this knowledge has got to be learned largely through the trial and error of watching not just the ball but each individual's stroke and racket movement.

One little trick of the Chinese expert is to mask his very fast service stroke (always with what seems to be the same hand motion but isn't), so his opponent can't tell whether the ball has topspin, backspin, sidespin, or no spin on it. Ordinarily such a penholder uses only one side of his racket, but sometimes, over his wooden, unused side, he has a special sheet of rubber just for serving.

Before he serves, he keeps his racket hidden under the table, twirls it or doesn't twirl it, then brings it up fast, executes his masked quick stroke and immediately on his follow-through drops the racket under the table again. This stratagem is very difficult for an uninitiate receiver to get used to—he's not conditioned to it and his timing is thrown off.

Sometimes, too, the server will vary his pace—will keep the ball on his palm longer than at other times. Sometimes at the last minute he'll change the speed or the direction of the ball (not very clever players often too obviously look where they're *not* going to serve). The Japanese player, Furukawa, occasionally begins a serve with the edge of his racket straight out at his opponent. He doesn't hit the ball on the edge but for a disconcerting moment it looks as if he will.

Often, if caught by surprise, you can be intimidated by unusual serves. Sometimes a grimace, a grunt, a foot stomp, an elaborate follow-through, can suggest that the server has put a great deal of spin on the ball—when just the opposite is true.

One New York opponent of mine, a very good defensive player, used to stand 6 feet back of the table and send a loaded chop serve at me that he'd perfected to land just over the net. He'd anticipate that I would try to drop it and would be rushing in as I, feeling the threat of his onrush, would have to be very careful not to watch him but the ball—else I'd set it up high enough for him to pick-hit away. This serve was a good psychological ploy. Supposedly I had all the advantage with the server so far back from the table. Why then could I never score the point outright? Why did I foolishly lose my "advantage"? Because, though it took me the longest time to understand it, I never had the advantage, not with that particular serve coming at me, not against that particular player.

Some coaches advocate having an ace-in-the-hole serve that is not shown until the very last moment when all depends on it. Others suggest trying out your repertoire of serves early. If it's obvious your opponent can't handle a certain serve, you're to save it for a possible tough spot. The fact that your opponent knows the serve is coming again will work on him so he'll feel added pressure and will perhaps force more than he should—naturally to his further disadvantage.

Some coaches say that, if you win the toss, you ought to choose to serve first. Since it's an accepted fact that the server has the advantage, you're presumably off to a good start. It's been my experience, though, that you ought to have your opponent serve first. If the game is close, you'll be serving at the end. Also, you have the psychological edge if you're coming from behind. Incidentally, if you're down 20-15 or 19-16 at game's end, I believe in attacking. Don't lose heart for a moment and don't play long points.

Advice To Receiver

If you're receiving serve, take some consolation in the fact that if you split points 50-50 on your opponent's serve, most coaches would say you're doing very well.

Of course, the receiver, like the server, can practice deception. With his two different sheets of rubber, he, too, can keep his racket under the table, then bring it into position precisely as the server must look to contact the ball. Sometimes the receiver can wait until the server's spin starts to wear off, and then at the last second can return the ball up from under the table with spin of his own. Or the receiver can vary his position a little, can at first appear not to be ready to attack, then fast get into position precisely as the server looks at the ball. I've heard it said you're never supposed to try to win the point outright off your opponent's serve—but if I anticipate correctly and get a serve to hit, I don't care what anybody says, I'm going to hit it.

Often the unexpected return wins you points. Several years ago I was leading Derek Wall, the former Canadian Champion 20-12 when (sometimes it happens, play every point though you might) he caught up and deuced the score at 20-20. Throughout the match, Derek had been giving me short chop serves, which I couldn't risk hitting—much as I wanted to—because there just wasn't any percentage in it. But now as Derek was about to serve I sensed that since he was momentarily out of danger (naturally I now needed not one point to win but two) he might not be quite as careful with this chop serve I'd never tried to hit. So I made up my mind that no matter how the ball would come over I was going to hit it. And as he served I moved with a two-step fast into position and, yes, it was a little high and I socked it perfect right into his mid-section and he never even got his racket on it. Then I followed with a serve-and-one and saved the game.

The Chinese, particularly, are very good at training their players to be aggressive, rather than play safe, during the late stages of a game. Of course this always demands a keen sense of anticipation. And since even a good player can be fooled, you've got to try to think like your opponent and anticipate not only his stroke but what's in his mind. As in poker, so in table tennis—the psychology of the moment must be considered. Hasegawa has pointed out that a man short of breath, lacking the energy or the desire for the moment to get into any long counter-driving exhange, is apt not to serve deep but short—for unconsciously he wants to get the point serve-and-one over with quickly.

DON'T PRACTICE MECHANICALLY

The kind of quick movements you're so apt to have to make in a tournament match you should first shadow-practice by yourself, then try out in a practice game. Surbek, who prefers to play a little farther back from the table than most Europeans, actually invites a short serve. But he knows from his shadow practice, from his practice games, as well as his tournament matches, just how much time he's got to crouch and spring toward the ball. So when he receives such a serve he literally jumps with both feet maybe a yard in close to the end line, gets his right shoulder way down almost to table level and skillfully pushes the ball back.

Whether defending or attacking you need first to anticipate well and move ever faster into your best possible stroke position, then (so you're not trying to smack the ball on the run) be able to stop and quickly ready yourself to come into the ball aggressively rather than wait passively for it to come to you. You must also practice stroke deception, have different last-minute ways of making contact with the ball, so your opponent can't prepare his counter-stroke ahead of time as you go into your backswing. Also, you must train yourself instinctively to return to your basic position even after you hit in your strongest shots—for your best opponents will return many of these and, as you'll soon find out, unless you immediately follow up your advantage you might not get another chance to.

You should play lots of practice games but not with the purpose of relentlessly winning them all. During these games you should try to serve, block, push, or drive shots to specific spots on the table —especially deep, to the corners. Try to keep in mind, too, that many opponents are weak in their mid-section. Indeed, I just recently heard one player complain that the white center line ought to be painted orange so that the white ball couldn't get "lost" when it came at him fast down the middle.

I personally am against mechanical practice. It's true it makes for machinelike efficiency (at least in practice), but I don't want my humanity neutralized. So I don't practice with a robot. I don't want to hit 100, let alone 1,000, forehands in a row. For me, the fun of playing is to engage occasionally with the unexpected, to improvise if need be, to keep my imagination fertile. You can no more play this game with just a percentage table or a list of do's and don'ts than you can bridge or poker. Adaptability allows you to survive in the table tennis arena as

120

Judy Bochenski of the U.S. Team (left) aggressively smacking one in against Canadian Champ Violetta Nesukaitis. (Photo by Mal Anderson)

elsewhere, and you don't psychically learn to be adaptable by relying solely on making yourself mechanically perfect.

PREPARING FOR A TOURNAMENT MATCH

Practice games, especially against different opponents, allow you to consciously and unconsciously make your own individual synthesis of a style. The only thing that's more helpful for your game is to play in tournaments—where against opponents going all-out your weaknesses are made apparent to you, perhaps for the first time.

This is not to say you shouldn't strategically practice some repetitious pattern plays—so long as you're not a slave to them. It also helps to keep a "book" on matches you've played where patterns have proved effective. (Compare a golfer visualizing his opponent, the course, which will trap him unless he's careful to map it, to position himself correctly.) Hence a coach might say to you, "Look, be smart. Last time you worked it out, remember? You have to go forehand-to-forehand with this guy, then you quick gotta angle one over to his back-

121

hand, then another one fast back to his forehand. Now he's gonna drop back and you can step in and hit him in the guts. O.K.?''

Or take the match the Canadian Champ Errol Caetano played against Danny Seemiller, our American number one, in the '74 Canadian Open. Errol, twirling his bat at the ready, had been slow-looping Danny in a successful effort to give himself time to station himself in one of those little pockets he likes 3 feet or so back from the table. If he could keep the ball in play to Seemiller's backhand, Danny couldn't counter hard enough or angle the ball quickly enough to the corners because he, Caetano, with his long arms, would already be there in control.

During a break in their match, one of Danny's friends (call him a coach if you like), a fellow team member Danny had confidence in, convinced him that he should serve to Caetano's backhand and begin as usual to counter the ball back to where Errol was waiting, only should then suddenly return the ball short with that soft, dead antispin touch shot he's so good at, should then keep moving Caetano in and out like this until soon Errol, reaching in, would have to pop the ball up at least a little, and then Danny could hit in.

This strategy worked, was duly recorded by both Seemiller and Caetano, and with some variation would surely come back into play the next time they faced one another—with of course the burden on Errol to prevent Danny from winning points in much the same manner again.

Players like Seemiller and Caetano who play table tennis weekend after weekend sometimes have trouble getting up for their matches. Therefore (there's no hard and fast rule about this) they may or may not practice the day before a tournament. Whatever helps them to keep their desire at a peak, that's what they'll do. Lesser players don't want to go stale either, but generally they'll prefer the ''security'' of playing the few days just before the tournament, so they'll feel that, well, they've done all they could to help them pull off the upset over the weekend. Since so much of the preparation is really psychological, whatever makes each player most at peace with himself, that's what he ought to do.

CONDUCT DURING A TOURNAMENT MATCH

Of course it helps if, as you come out for your first match, you've al-

Danny Seemiller, U.S. number 1, playing Canadian Champ Errol Caetano in the '74 Canadian Open at Toronto. (Photo by Mal Anderson)

ready acquired sufficient tournament confidence to feel good. Naturally such a positive feeling is not going to come from just practicing mechanically or playing against a few opponents of limited ability. It can only be developed by proving yourself under fire. However, with the right equipment, the right playing outfit, you can always look like a professional—and that's worth at least a few points to start off with.

Also, win or lose (and of course tournaments are arranged so that you can play not just in one event but several round robin or elimination events over the weekend), you can try hard to preserve your initial freshness in the matches that follow your first one. Before you're called to play again, you ought to leave the immediate tournament area for some fresh air and come back with a more eager eye towards playing. You ought also to change shirt, socks, underpants after every strenuous match or two or even at the 5-minute break in the middle of a match. Of course in actual practice this is much too much trouble for the great majority of players and so there's nothing fresh about most of them.

If it happens that your first- or even second-round opponent isn't so good, you should quite seriously practice putting the ball in that spot where he's best. The charismatic New York star, Marty Reisman, used to go the full 5 games in a best 3-out-of-5 game match with players he could give at least 12 points a game to—and make everybody enjoy it.

Marty would always come out looking very dapper, very cool and fresh—never sweaty as if from having frantically practiced at the last minute. His early round matches would be his warm-up, and he'd always start with simple, easy strokes that created the impression he was full of confidence and perfectly happy and at peace with himself out there. People marveled at his table control—they saw reflected in it, they wanted to see reflected in it, the heroic ideal of his own self-control—and Marty soon came to think no less of it himself. In his table tennis theater, he was for me and my generation an archetypal figure—the artist-magician—who, with just a little spin of the ball here, a little there, could make our weekend world seem much more magical, and therefore much more real and meaningful, than for most of our lives we in fact knew it to be.

Be Self-Possessed, Analytical

This quality of self-possession is an extremely valuable one for a table tennis player. Here's John Tannehill talking about the strategy of self. (He was a very inquiring teenager on our mind-blowing "Ping-Pong diplomacy" trip to China.) "A real student of the sport doesn't get upset. Instead, he says, 'I will overcome.' A student is always asking questions in his head. This is what I try to do in table tennis. My opponent—is he going to serve short? Long? With what kind of spin? Am I going to receive him like last time? If I hit a ball to my opponent's backhand and it goes in for a winner, is he next time going to be psychologically covering that spot and so leave open his middle? If these questions don't come into my head, then my game dies—because I'm mentally dead."

Not just John (who as a student of yoga could also have some balancing things to say about the unconscious life of the body) but many another strategic player is invariably looking for psychological vantage points that might help him win a match. For instance, if immediately after your opponent makes a mistake or two he is not thinking well, it's quite possible that if you really concentrate you can "break" him and the game wide open then and there.

Sometimes, if you can just win one key point, the 13-11 point, say, you have turned the outcome decidedly in your favor. One thing to always remember when you're ahead, though, is to fight even harder. This is especially true when you're leading 2 games to 1 in a best 3-out-of-5-game match against a favored opponent. For at this point, you've won a little victory of sorts and are apt to unconsciously want to accept the reward you've not yet earned.

Whether you're playing a 2-out-of-3 or 3-out-of-5-game match, the first game is clearly most important. As are the first 10 points—though against a weaker player a bad start may urge you to play harder. You and your coach should study statistically how you win points —whether in bunches or tit for tat. If you're a streaky player, it doesn't matter so much, so long as you don't get discouraged, whether you're 3 or 4 points down even at mid-game.

Some coaches think you ought to play cautiously when you begin a match against a new opponent—that you ought to try to get the feel of his game, how he spins the ball, how he tries to disguise his spin, how he follows up or fails to follow up certain shots. But I myself like to come out swinging.

I opened up strong in Japan against former World Champion Sido in the 1971 World Jubilee Cup (for players over 40) and when the balls went in I won. But in the final against the Czech Stipek, another ex-world-class player, I never did get started right. He swung outrageously at the first 5 balls and I led 5-0. But somehow thereafter, though in the beginning I even tried risking some smashes myself (almost like a chess player equalizing back his won material for better psychological position), my balls didn't go in and I ended up much of the match on defense—as if unconsciously intimidated by those first fearless swings of my opponent.

Better, then, from my experience to right away try to force your opponent to get used to you. Why play a waiting game? Better to have your head very clear at the outset about what you want to do— and do it.

Naturally when you're winning, you don't change your strategy. I remember in the '74 U.S. Open when Dell Sweeris, one of our best players, was playing the number-one Indian Niraj Bajaj. Dell had been looping slow, been spinning slow and deep, and winning points that way, but then, 20-19 match point up, had followed his natural instinct to go for the one shot to win, had looped fast, and Bajaj had quickly blocked the ball to Dell's backhand, and, winning that point, had then run out the match.

If you're losing, however, most players feel you've got to try something different—at least change the pace of the game. Some very good players when they're off form are notorious for their stalling tactics —will walk to retrieve the ball very slowly, take time out to comb their hair, wipe real or imaginary specks off the table, look (hand on hips) high to heaven then curse themselves or their opponent, go for their towel, and so on—prepare to serve, then hesitate, give their opponent a baleful stare, wait, wait, then finally serve.

Keep Your Temper

The defense against all this nonsense is to keep a poker face and never—and I mean never—take your eye off the ball, so as to keep your perfect concentration.

Naturally sometimes you do have to tie your shoelaces or clean the sweat from your glasses, and sometimes certain ploys—like going for your towel—used sparingly are not considered out of line by many good players, especially when, by an implied mutual consent, both of you are equally guilty of delaying the game. Some Europeans —Stipancic of Yugoslavia, for example, who has quite a temper— have this little trick, if the game is close and they want to stall, of reaching out to retrieve the ball and then accidentally on purpose hitting it with their bat still farther away to give themselves more time to try to get composed. Or you can try this: if, in a 3-out-of-5-game match, you're getting beat bad, you can begin deliberately throwing away points, playing like a beginner, in the hope of disrupting your opponent's timing in the games to come.

What really makes you mad, though, because it's obviously cheating, and where you need a coach or friend to speak up for you, is when a player purposefully serves a "wet" ball—for then no stroke can work its proper effect and the ball will uncontrollably slide off your

126

racket right down onto the table and into the net. Or you can understandably be infuriated as I was once when I was playing a 3-time National Champion and after I'd won the first game and was leading 12-5 in the second he broke the ball.

"Keep your temper," said the Caterpillar to Alice—and it's generally good advice, in Wonderland or anywhere else. Certainly you won't be able to play table tennis when you're so angry you can't see straight—you won't want to control yourself or your reflexes. I know, I've seen players so mad they've torn the rubber off their paddles right out there at the table.

I don't mean to say, though, that you have to be a robot. If you begin to feel the pressure, if you feel tight, blow out air. If you want to yell encouragement to yourself during the match and raise your clenched fist high, why not do it—at least until an umpire tells you to cool it. In fact, I myself think it's all right for you even to express anger. That hookah-smoking Caterpillar, after all, was as much provocateur as guru. If you're getting upset, why keep all that tension bottled up inside? But you must have the self-control, the discipline, to see that your momentary outburst doesn't keep you from mentally and physically being ready to play the next point to the very best of your ability.

Self-disgust is very often even an excellent player's downfall. You just cannot give into that—not even for one point.

Of course you've got to take all this moralizing as pretty much a general rule. Strange things sometimes happen. I remember a match in the Eastern Open some years ago, played under the Expedite Rule, where at 19-all in the deciding game the umpire claimed an irregularity, a foul—said one of the players had moved the table. The offending player denied it vigorously, exchanged words with the umpire, then, still steaming, resumed play. His opponent, of course, seeing this player upset, was quick to serve—and, sure enough, the player who was blind mad didn't even look, just swatted the ball as hard as he could. Only, miraculously, on its rocketed way to the stands, it correctly hit the other side of the table. Deuce! The crowd went crazy—it was the greatest shot they'd ever seen. And, having gotten that spasm of rage out, the offending player immediately took hold of himself and went on to win the next two points over his stunned opponent, who was practically paralyzed at not being given the match.

EXPEDITE RULE

This match I just described was played under the Expedite Rule. What does that mean? Well, many years ago, in order to stop two defensive players (neither of whom could hit very well) from "chiseling" forever, the USTTA made a rule (put into effect for the rest of the match at the precise moment any game has lasted 15 minutes) that says the server must win the point by the time he's served and then stroked the ball 12 more times over the net. That is, if the opponent makes 13 valid returns, *he* automatically wins the point. In this variation the serve alternates. And since the burden is on the server to score the point, it's sometimes good strategy for the receiver to roll the ball and so make it harder for the server to take over the offense and get his shot in. At any rate, it's generally not considered very smart to get desperate and try to bang the ball in before your 10th shot. This is not an easy rule to play under even for those who have had some experience with it, and unless you're just absolutely stymied by your opponent's defense I don't recommend pushing yourself into it.

One celebrated world champion, a sort of law unto himself, supposedly used to bring 3 chess clocks to be put under the playing table, timed to go off at intervals that would warn him if and when his match might go expedite. Why one opponent after another wasn't alarmed by them, the story didn't say. Perhaps they wanted to know the same information?

A COACH, A TEACHER, CAN HELP

A coach repeatedly needs to be alert to any kind of irregularity in the play. In the 1969 U.S. Open Team Championships, the former National Champion Bobby Gusikoff is leading his opponent 18-17 in a very important game. As he's about to serve, he looks at the umpire, who's obliged to call both the score and the name of the server before the ball is put into play. But then before the umpire can finish his call ("18-17 . . ."), Gusikoff, too anxious, half serves, half tries to hold the ball, and so puts it into the net. Whereupon the umpire awards the point to Gusikoff's opponent, says it's "18-all."

128

This was a bad ruling, though, because had the serve been good the umpire would have called a "let"—and therefore since there was no way for Gusikoff to have won the point he shouldn't have been held accountable for its loss. But at the time neither Bobby nor anyone acting as his coach thought to protest the point—and Gusikoff's New York team lost the Championship.

Though a player may receive advice from his coach after a game, he is not supposed to receive any such information during a game. However, this practice is not often held to, not even at world championships. I know a coach who used to work out signals with his player-daughter. And in a very hushed moment out there when the score was close, you'd suddenly hear his intense, preoccupied voice yell out, "66, Honey!"

On some occasions a coach had best say nothing. Once in a tournament in Miami, my older boy was down 19-11 and just kept hitting in shots until the game drew even—at which point the odds on him hitting in still more shots were prohibitive. Still, I could do nothing but hold my breath lest I break the magic spell—and he finished with two winners.

It helps if the coach constantly observes the player, so that whenever the player looks over, the coach is watching him. I've always done this with my two sons because I've always wanted them to feel strongly that every point is important. I've always disliked it if, when they have an easy match, they aren't serious about their play. I know that you have to work at being mentally tough, that if you're loose and sloppy one match it may not be easy to regain your concentration to play the next one well.

This doesn't mean, though, that you always have to look like the Japanese coach and all the players on his bench at a world team championship. There, when a Japanese player misses an easy one, what we call a "hanger," and looks back at his teammates, they're all nodding affirmatively, as if in approval, as if he'd just hit the shot in. I never could figure out why that Japanese player on missing the ball looks back. What does he expect to see? Perhaps he'd unconsciously prefer just once some show of even public displeasure from his coach and teammates?

It's true, though, that the player can often draw psychic help from his teammates and even the spectators. At world championships Sweden's Johansson is spurred on by his supporters in all parts of the stands—they yodel. In Jamaica, when someone comes from behind to

1975 World Doubles Champion Gabor Gergely of Hungary following through. Instantly recognizable is Hungarian Coach Berzcik with white towel and dark glasses and notebook in hand ready with advice. (Photo by Mike Hoffland)

Table tennis
warrior-intellectual-zen
archer John Tannehill of
the U.S.A. (Photo by
Mal Anderson)

even the score, everyone in the stadium wildly applauds. Here in the
U.S., one of our own very best players has said, "It's impossible to
play without spectators. They give energy to the table and to the whole
concept of the sport."

Self-Mobilization

Of course much depends, too, on your own self-mobilization. After
the match—win or lose—you must ask yourself this leadoff question,
"What have I learned from playing against this opponent?" And then
record your follow-up questions and answers, your observations, in a
notebook. Or—I've seen it done—you might adhesive-tape the handle
of your racket with little written directives for the matches to come
(which might suggest to strangers only that you're collecting the auto-
graphs of those players who at the present time are beating you).

In this yin-yang of a physical yet very intellectual sport it helps if
you have your own heroes to guide you. They need not be table tennis
players to offer you inspiration in any sphere of life that interests you.
Here's young John Tannehill sharing his thoughts with us again.

131

"One writer who's helped me become a better student and so a better table tennis player is Carlos Castaneda. After reading him, I like to think of myself as a warrior, as a man of unbending intent. A warrior never indulges himself, never complains. He chooses a path with heart, and never doubts himself. He never looks back—like Dr. Faustus, who both wanted his pact with the devil and didn't.

"Kierkegaard says the same thing. Says purity of heart is to will one thing and then follow that path with passion, without doubt or remorse. Each table tennis shot I make, I quite consciously want to be a symbol of that."

STRATEGY IN PLAYING DOUBLES

I'm including a brief discussion of doubles play here as sort of an appendix to this chapter, because doubles really does demand from you and your partner some well thought out strategy and the same kind of good, understanding relationship I'd expect you to have with your coach.

I've always enjoyed playing doubles—both men's and mixed—and since at one time or other I've partnered just about every top player in the country, I've always fancied myself better at it than at singles. The most important thing in doubles (where of course you alternate shots) is to play with a regular partner whom you have confidence in, even when for the moment he or she's not playing well, and whose game complements your own.

Naturally I've always played well with another steady, stay-at-the-table blocker and hitter—like 3-time U.S. Open Champion Patty Martinez of California. We've always handled our assigned half of the table well, in mirror fashion, have each always followed up any advantage the other may have gained. And, most important, we've always had a good 50-50 understanding in that when she's killing the ball well I look to set her up, and vice versa.

A combination much sought after in this or any era is a good left-hander playing with an equally good right-hander. For, like the '73 World Doubles Champions, Bengtsson and Johansson, both stay out of each other's way and continually force a forehand attack.

When two right-handers play together, the server can try to serve

Author embracing his partner, three-time U.S. Champ Patty Martinez of California, after their win over the English Men's Champion Denis Neale and his partner Canadian Champ Violetta Nesukaitis in Toronto, Fall, 1968.

Author and his partner, U.S. Team Member Judy Bochenski, in 1974 Canadian Open Mixed Doubles final against Danny Seemiller and In Sook Na. (Photo by Mal Anderson)

Kjell Johansson (left) and Stellan Bengtsson, 1973 World Doubles Champions, keeping on their toes against arch rivals Anton Stipancic (third from left) and Dragutin Surbek of Yugoslavia. (Photo by Mal Anderson)

backhand to give his partner more forehand room. Short chop and sidespin is best, mixed from time to time with no spin and topspin serves. Rarely serve long, for that ball can be too aggressively returned. Though naturally you must serve from your forehand box into your opponent's (of course, only the serve initially starting the point need be placed diagonally), you can, on occasion, vary your address. If you and your partner prefer a more centered position, you can serve, especially a short right-to-left sidespin serve, from just to the right side of the middle line and then, instead of moving right, can go left as your partner comes in behind you.

Just as serving is important, so too is receiving. If the pair makes a mistake in the beginning, they will be even less able than in singles to right themselves. The ball will be quickly looped or angled away. Again it's helpful if one receiver can take the ball backhand to give his partner more forehand room. I prefer to take the ball on my forehand, though, because if I can read the spin correctly, I can make the desired

134

Doubles action between (left to right) Danny Seemiller and Joe Rokop
of Pittsburgh (far side of table) and Alexander Shiroky and Sam Ham-
mond of New York in a tournament at the Philadelphia Table Tennis
Club. (Photo by Mal Anderson)

much more forceful return—then, as I follow through, can continue
moving to my left and then come back in a semicircle to hit the ball
again after my partner's taken his shot.

Seizing the initiative and staying out of your partner's way are both
musts. How you both do this successfully, of course, is your own business. Some partnerships prefer to stand very close to one another,
with their looper or hitter positioned in the background and their
blocker half shuttling laterally back and forth with expert timing as his
own partner's shot just grazes by him.

The idea, finally, for you and your partner is to use as little unneces-
sary movement as possible as each of you takes turns trying to wrest an
advantage from the one opponent whose ball is easier to hit or loop
than the other's. (This is possible, of course, because the order, the
specific opponent you're stroking the ball at, changes after every game
and when one partnership reaches 10 in the final game.)

Doubles, then, as you can begin to see, is a very strategic game.

Dell and Connie Sweeris in 1970 on winning one of their U.S. Mixed Doubles Championships. (Photo by William Scheltema)

Sometimes, for example, when you can't help yourself and are back on defense, and your partner is hopelessly out of position, it's not enough for you to return the ball as you would in singles—you must take a chance and, though the shot isn't at all to your liking, must go all out to try to score the point.

You and your partner, remember, are constantly trying to prevent either of those players opposite you from taking their best shots. To this end, both of you are attempting to control the table by placing the ball, often successively to the same pinpointed area, so that one of your opponents at least will be drawn out of position and thus be incapable of getting set for a good shot. At which point, you'll naturally come in and seize the initiative. Of course, you can recognize the importance of having a coach in doubles, too, for he will be able to work out on-the-spot pattern plays that will allow you and your partner to take advantage of your opponents' weaknesses.

chapter seven

Y ou remember in the last Basic Strokes chapter I was telling you that there are not now nearly so many choppers, especially deep choppers, as in years gone by. Their back-from-the-table style is not well suited to the continuing advances of the spin game. Therefore most of today's players who don't want to chop, who even want to attack but who can't always withstand all the varied spins of their equally aggressive counterparts, have had to find new ways to counter the loop, this strange, down-under, kangaroo of a shot.

THE LOB

One stroke they've come up with, followed through with, is the lob.

advanced play

This is a very high, balloonlike lift shot that's begun anywhere off your back foot from the shoelaces up to the knees, 15-20 feet from deep behind the table.

It may happen sometimes with an expert lobber like Secretin of France or Surbek or Hasegawa (the wiry Japanese half squatting, then, like a weight lifter, raising up the heavily-spun ball that's come to his backhand center), that the swaying high-rise lob he makes is stronger than his opponent's drive. But the shot was really devised with defense in mind, to take the place of a chop, even against a vanishing flat hitter—for neither against today's powerful, very spinny sidespin loop or a no-spin, flat-power hit from the past can you really chop the ball hard enough to be sure of winning the point.

One advantage of the lob shot is the time it gives you, especially if

Rory Brassington, the best lobber in the U.S., back on his right foot preparatory to lifting the ball up and away. (Photo by Mal Anderson)

you can anticipate your opponent's moves well, to get back into position. Another is that this ball is always going to bounce very high on your opponent's side, so high that it will be harder than most people think—and virtually impossible for a beginner to hit with any accuracy short of setting a shot up for your opponent. Still another advantage is that even if your aim is off a little (and with all the variables it often is—maybe, for example, your lob isn't as deep as you want it), you can

Surbek eyeing the ball, about to lob it back from the barrier. (Photo by Mike Hoffland)

still send the ball right to where your opponent is waiting and the sometimes unpredictable spin on it will make it harder to handle than a chop and of course impossible to loop.

How successful the lob's been as a substitute for chop, though, is highly questionable. The trouble is that, whereas a chopper can return the ball again and again—it seems forever—the lobber cannot. (Perhaps, because of the too-low ceilings in many a club, there's been

141

Yugoslavia's Surbek "catching" a ball and lobbing it back as Sweden's Johansson, expecting the unbelievable return, waits in readiness to hammer in another smash. (Photo by Mal Anderson)

little chance to really practice the shot?) No, thrill the crowd though he might—like a baseball player with his great catches half into the stands, desperate "catches" that the lobber must then somehow, without looking, forehand or backhand forcefully flip 20 feet in the air back over his head—he can't keep it up.

Also, the lob is always high enough to hit. And hit and hit and hit. And, as the Japanese pips-out attacker Kohno can demonstrate, it can be devastatingly smother-killed with a crouching, flat, in-over-the-table stroke of shoulder height that whips into the ball as, ready to accelerate, it hops its first six inches over the net.

MEDIUM TO FAST BACK-FROM-THE-TABLE LOOP

Ideally, the best defense against any kind of topspin is offense. Therefore it may be best if you don't drop as far back from the table as a lobber, but move into a sort of mid-ground and, while waiting for an opening of your own against a strong attacker, adopt what you might call either a loop offense or a loop defense.

I of course don't play this way because (1) I'm not a spinner and (2) I prefer the in-fighting at the table. But more and more of the great European stars, instead of pushing (as in the old days) are now using heavy topspin to get into position. However, because there's so much potential for topspin on the ball nowadays, you've got to be very careful about your timing. Often as you come to meet the ball, it'll not only bounce lower than you at first think, but, especially on fast tables, it'll be apt to skid. A good thing, then, that maybe you're back away from the table to see and better take the spin.

Surbek's Loop

Perhaps one of the best heavy topspin techniques to begin describing to you is the Yugoslav Surbek's. He's a marvelous lobber and so is often far back from the table. But he's also one of the best counter-loopers in the world, particularly from 20 feet out, and so even if he's in trouble is always a threat to take over the positional advantage that both looper and counter-looper are always hopping and pushing chess pieces for.

For the sake of illustration, then, Surbek could be 3 feet back of the table on his backhand side or several feet farther out. At any event, he waits at-the-forehand-ready there at the diamond-point table edge, at a juncture of his thigh and crotch. He has a wide stance of about 2½ feet, his right foot has been brought back and to the side, and he is up on both toes.

As the ball comes into the forehand center he's made for himself, he bends down on his right leg while his left one, stretched out for balance, seems reluctant to leave its original position. His left arm, swung round almost parallel with the center line of the table, looks as if its companion arm, the one that's deceptively not as noticeable, that's doing all the work, is about to throw a spear into the heart of his opponent.

Surbek's racket is brought far back and down, only six inches or so from the floor, beyond his bent right knee, so that the forehand face of it may even be flat down, with the top of the blade pointing away from the oncoming ball. His outstretched left foot skids away from its held-

Surbek's forehand loop. (Photo sequence by Chui Fan Liu)

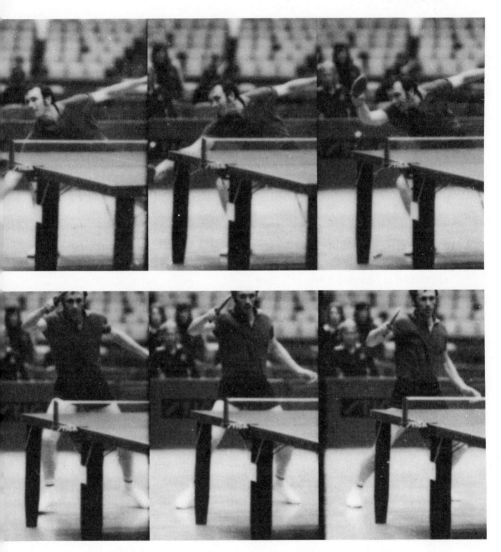

to position and now all his weight is up on the ball of his right foot as he starts to spring and bring the head of his closed racket around and up. His whole body, not just his arm, swings in well below table height as he wrist-snaps the ball forward in a heavy spin—and as he springs off his right leg, his left one comes over to hold and balance his weight. His follow-through goes up in a line parallel to the center line, so that he does not bring his body all the way around as in a smash.

Jonyer's Loop

1975 World Champion Jonyer, whose arms-down-and-hanging-loosely stance is like a great ape's, has a stroke something like Surbek's. But his left foot almost immediately leaves the floor, though just for a moment, because he takes his racket back farther behind him even than Surbek, back around farther than any player I've ever seen, almost in a line with his left foot.

Absolutely all his weight goes back on his right foot, preparatory to this leg's later push off the floor—that part of the loop technique devised to give added power as the player comes through the ball and which is often neglected by many a beginner. As Jonyer starts swooping upward and forward through, his left foot comes back down to its rolled right position. As he's still coming through, his bat closed, his left foot slides over and, for a discus-whirling moment, it seems he's leaning backward. Now his free left hand, which had spun right with him, has spun back again, and on he comes, ready at the last moment to snap his wrist as he stiffarms through and around and down until his left knee is dangerously close to knocking the floor.

Both Jonyer and his 1971 World Doubles Champion partner Tibor Klampar, in delivering their famous Hungarian top and sidespin loops, remind me of a bowler throwing hook after hook. As their weight goes back onto that right foot and they come up and forward into the outside part of the ball, they look as if they're about to fall backwards into a chair. This is because of their whirlaround action, typified in the very beginning of their stroke by their left, free hand that's swung so far over to the right it seems ready to catch the very ball they want to loop. Also, they need a fully extended arm when they power the ball through with their whole body.

1975 World Champion Jonyer's pickup and follow-through for his loop drive. (Photos by Mike Hoffland)

Jonyer on his discus-like way to meeting the ball in a whirl-around smash.
(Photo by Mike Hoffland)

Jonyer's almost falling-backwards follow-through.
(Photo by Mike Hoffland)

Surbek doing one of his lunging acrobatic splits.

Their 10-15 feet behind the table, long-armed, half-moon strokes, which back in 1971 people at first considered eccentric, allowed them to enlarge what experts thought of as the playing court. But although their incredibly curving sidespin loops can draw their opponents out of position (even great ones like Surbek might have to do a lunging acrobatic split), these same wide-arcing spin shots, which they delight in taking outside the sideline, the better to curve a ball spectacularly around the net, can also draw them out of position.

Jonyer's Backhand Loop

Jonyer, who's always trying to open the point, also has a very strong in-close-to-the-table backhand loop, a brief discussion of which I'm going to include here. Although this is one of the hardest shots in the game to learn, it is yet a very important one, for in the early '70s it al-

149

lowed the Europeans to challenge the 20-year-old Oriental dominance of the sport. A player, once having mastered this loop, can get out of the backhand corner he's often been locked into and can force from his diagonal opponent, who often won't be able aggressively to handle his topspin, the loose ball he's been waiting for to open his forehand.

Here's Jonyer's supple technique. He squats forward like a football center, and as the ball comes toward him, he brings the racket down under him as if he were about to hike a football and closes the blade until it's almost facing the floor. As the ball comes in close, he half encircles it with his free hand, lets the ball drop a bit more than usual, then twists up from his crotch and rocks back a little. As he comes through the ball, the tip of his elbow is much higher than his about-to-be-turned-over wrist.

Hasegawa's Loop

The Japanese, in addition to having some of the world's best choppers, also have very good loopers and smashers. Hasegawa's stance, his stroke, are a little different from the Europeans. When the ball comes into Hasegawa's backhand court he's already anticipated it and is standing at his forehand-ready far outside the sideline (especially far out considering he's a shakehands player and not a penholder). Since he's smaller than Surbek or Jonyer, his stance span is only about a foot and a half, and from his extreme position on the left side he has to be in very good shape to continuously move fast to cover his whole forehand court.

His right foot's sideways, like Surbek's, but it's still six inches outside the sideline. He brings his racket pretty far back—but, facing him, you can still see it, so it's not quite as far back as Surbek's and certainly it's not all the way around behind him on the other side like Jonyer's. Then a little stiffarmed, though not as much as Jonyer, he comes through and over, meets the ball about heart-high (higher than Surbek or Jonyer) at the top of its hop a foot or two behind the table. Throughout, his footwork—the right foot dropped back, the left one rolled, the power push off the right leg as he swings through and onto the rolled back left foot—is all standard. His follow-through finishes with the racket high-left past his head and perfectly squared-off with the end line, while his encircling free hand, emphasizing his perfect

150

1967 World
Champion
Hasegawa
balanced when
off balance.
Photo by
Neal Fox)

balance, comes symetrically over, so much so that if it, too, held a
racket the blades would become one.

JAPANESE FOREHAND DRIVE

In stroking any drive, you must lean into the ball, must get your wrist
into the shot. If you make contact well, the ball will often skid and, if
it's allowed to, shoot off your opponent's side of the table. As in golf,
you don't have to hurry your backswing, but your racket must be
squared-off coming through and you must accelerate fast just before
you hit the ball. Against a heavy chop, you open the racket and come
up and over. But against a no-spin block, you can't open the
racket—else the ball will fly off. Charlie Wuvanich, a world-class
player originally from Thailand, who's trained in Japan and who is
now one of our country's best coaches, urges his students to crouch
low and make their follow-through about even with the top of the net.

151

Surbek's perfect upward and forward finishing stroke for his loop drive. (Photo by Mike Hoffland)

The Japanese have a technique for their drives and smashes, which Wuvanich himself practices, whereby they literally stride or even bound in to kill the ball. The 1969 World Champion Shigeoh Itoh was able in the early '70s to get more speed on the ball by sort of exploding into his shot on the run—though, as you can imagine, if he didn't time his spring perfectly or if the ball were suddenly to take a strange spin or skid on the table, he might well be more like the dying animal, the killed, than the killer.

There is a distinction between the drive and the smash that may very easily be seen in the player's follow-through. With the old hard rubber bat, the kind I started using in 1950, the best players, in an effort to get more speed and hop into their shots, whipped their strokes forward and upward and could eye, could smartly salute, their follow-through.

Today, 25 years later, a player like Itoh, though he's ending his career (he's retired once, twice . . .), in an effort to get more speed and spin into his shots, is stiffarming the ball, stroking it upward and forward so that it looks like anything but a salute to old Time: after coming through, he finishes up as if he were reaching to put something away for good, along with his many trophies, on still another shelf of the 50-year-old history of our sport.

U.S. Team Member Peter Pradit smashes the ball so hard it seems to go through the net. (Photo by Mal Anderson)

U.S. number 1 Danny Seemiller in Benson and Hedges Invitational at Kingston, Jamaica. The force of Danny's smash has taken him over to his opponent's side of the table. (Photo courtesy of Tony Becca)

SMASH

Itoh's penholder smash is more representative. As he springs, makes contact after his long backswing and nearly straight-armed return towards the ball, his racket is perfectly squared-off. As the right side of his body swings round to follow the ball, his left foot slides a little left, then holds steady there because all his shifting weight from his waist movement has come crouched down on it. His right foot that he's pushed off from, sprung from, rolls left as his extended follow-through almost bumps his knee to the floor. He comes so close to getting it scraped, you wonder why he doesn't wear a knee protector like a basketball player. But then, as he maintains an expert balance, his racket just seems to unwrap itself from round his head and he springs back into readiness for his next shot.

The important things to remember in the hard-hit smash, as in the heavy spin loop, are that (1) your weight has to go from your left foot

153

Johansson's "Hammer." (Photo sequence by Chui Fan Liu)

back to your right one and that (2) as you rock or, like with the rapidly accelerating speed of your bat, rocket back in to make contact with the ball, your waist and torso must come full swing so that you'll finish very well.

Johansson's ''Hammer''

Johansson's shakehands forehand (''The Hammer'') is really not too different from Itoh's. His stance, like Surbek's, is very wide, spans virtually more than the whole of his backhand court. All 6'3'' of him stays at the backhand-ready and is much more willing now than 10 years ago to try to control play up at the table with his very consistent, straight counterdrive game. Finally, when he gets an opening, he virtually leaps at the ball with his forehand.

When he anticipates the opportunity for a smash coming, he does a quick two-step left until he's centered at the backhand diamond-point edge of the table. His left foot is rolled right and his weight, of course, is back on his right foot, which is pointing sideways. As he comes through with his squared-off racket, his arm is not stiff (like the loopers Surbek and Jonyer) but bent, close in—like the handle of a well pump—and his wrist is not at all up but even cocked a little back and

154

down. Up he goes on his right toe, suddenly leaps, and, both feet off the floor, a terrible grimace on his face (someone once told me you could tell a good player by the desire you saw in his face), he smacks the ball in as hard as he can.

His momentum, especially if it's a passing shot and he's given himself to it aesthetically, often angles him away from the table. Johansson's follow-through suggests he's wrapping a devil-may-care

Sweden's 1973 World Finalist Kjell Johansson grimacing in a hard backhand. It's this shot that often sets up his forehand "hammer" kill. (Photo by Mike Hoffland)

Johansson's somewhat subdued, feet-still-on-the-floor forehand drive. Still, it looks like he hit it hard enough to hurt. (Photo by Mike Hoffland)

scarf round his neck. And many times he couples his swing through with a strangely, even comically brought out forefinger on his curled-in free hand (strange, that is, until you notice it points precisely parallel with his forearm pump), a complementary forefinger—as if in hitting in one of his deceptive shots he's ironically trying to tell his bewildered opponent, "It went thataway."

BENGTSSON'S IN-CLOSE-TO-THE-TABLE STYLE

Johansson's famous Swedish teammate, the former World Singles and Doubles Champion Stellan Bengtsson, hasn't the forehand follow-through of any of the bigger 6-footers because, though on occasion he can, he doesn't usually loop hard or hit hard. Instead, this mercurial left-hander depends on his exceptionally fine footwork, on moving, moving, moving, constantly pressing an in-close-to-the-table loop attack or constantly staving off one by countering or blocking.

Like many other European and Chinese (but not Japanese) players, he stands rather close to the middle of the table. Perhaps because he's a steady spinner rather than an all-out hitter or smasher, he's very good at following his often well-disguised serves with an indefatigable top-spin.

Moving quickly into position to loop, he takes the ball at his back-hand corner deep down below the knee with a very closed racket. As he readies himself to make contact, he coils in his right shoulder and free, balancing hand (almost as if he were holding—who knows what?—an imaginary plant in it), then, as he's about to rub the ball upward and forward, he pushes off his back left leg—left leg because he's left-handed. His follow-through, though complete, is much shorter than those of the big swingers I've discussed earlier (up so close to the table like that, it's all he has time for, especially against a fast pusher or blocker). After he loops the ball in, he immediately moves centerward to press whatever advantage he can from either wing.

In one of our recent U.S. Opens, I saw Bengtsson play a match against the Japanese defensive star Takashima, and his pattern of attack against that style was typical. First, he would serve fast to get Takashima to chop. Then, with his heavy sponge bat, the kind most dif-

Bengtsson's forehand loop and kill. (Photo sequence by Chui Fan Liu)

ficult to control, he'd pick up his forehand and begin to vary the spin of his little loop, then drop the ball, maybe push it (though here he had to be very careful, for Takashima, a great pick-hitter, would come in and hit anything that was the least little bit too high). Then take up the top-spin again, never looping the ball hard, never driving it. Eventually, if Takashima didn't miss—and he usually didn't—Bengtsson would find the opening and make quite a few more kill shots than he'd miss.

Sounds simple compared to all the whirlaround power play I've been describing? Maybe so. But to be that steady, have that kind of

continued on pages 160 & 161

control, is to show quite an advance from those days he quit high school and went to Japan to do nothing but train to be the World Champion he dreamed he could become.

Of course Bengtsson's equally good on receiving serve, keeping the ball short so his opponent can't get in below the ball to spin it at him. This then often allows him to take over the forehand topspin attack even after an opponent's serve into his backhand corner.

Bengtsson also has a unique backhand block—the racket's held up like a lollipop—which is very effective, especially for short touch

159

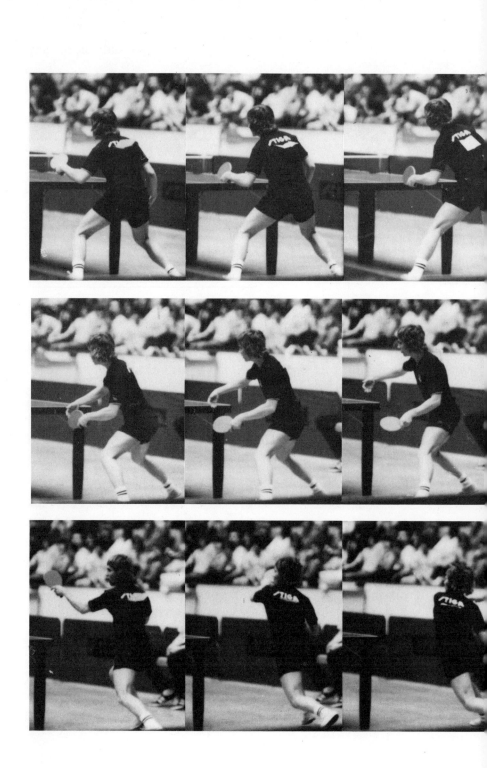

shots. Surbek and Jonyer, for instance, are not great blockers, so if Bengtsson can draw them into the table, he can then, still keeping his racket upright, force them back out again, and in the process follow with his own very consistent forehand.

One last point about this former world champion's game. Steady though it is, it's not dull. All that kinetic energy of his makes for something unexpected and electrical.

In the 1975 Canadian Open International Team Matches in Quebec, I saw Bengtsson 20-18 match point down to the Yugoslav Zlatko Cordas. The young Swede served and seemingly without taking any backswing at all snapped in a return that poor Cordas could only snort ironically at. In some mysterious way that I couldn't even see, let alone do, he apparently pivoted power into the ball from a slight turn in his wrist. At any event, he followed that point winner with another—and of course went on to win the match.

CHINESE JAB-BLOCKER

My aim when I started out in this chapter was to lob up for all to see those sophisticated away-from-the-table shots that the inverted racket has made possible in recent years. I find now that I've done this but at the same time have been steadily moving back closer and closer to the net—until I'm rather back where I began a few chapters ago with the blocker. The pips-out blocker it may even be, who's always kept very busy, on the ball, trying to outmaneuver his opponent, putting one deep to his forehand this way, putting a little one up short to his backhand that way.

Of course it isn't enough for you, as you get better, to make more or less defensive blocks, even very carefully placed ones. In the hands of experts these are used mostly against kills or super loops—almost as a form of self-defense. No, you have to learn to be a "jabber" like those great Chinese penholders Li Ching-kuang and Hsi En-ting (though it used to be in the old days that when somebody "jabbed" a ball they couldn't play at all). This means you have to forget about those delicate "touch" blocks I myself get great enjoyment out of playing.

To "jab" the ball you adapt a squared-off, rocklike stance right up at the table. Your feet are firmly planted under the table (perhaps with a little more weight on the right foot than the left) and your knees are forward, bent directly under the endline. The upper part of your body, particularly your right shoulder, is leaning in over the table, while your arm is very stiffly, forcefully, thrusting the racket in a forward, downward motion in whatever direction you wish—though only through trial and error can you find just the right angle racket and force to keep from hitting the ball off the table or into the net. The jab, in other words, is like a block with a short, six inch or so, follow-through. I know, I told you right at the very beginning not to do this. Well, it wouldn't have worked for you then, it may not work for you now. But keep experimenting. What have you got to lose?

OLD QUESTION: PIPS-OUT OR PIPS-IN RUBBER?

As the history of table tennis shows, a number of very good players over the years have consistently changed the rubber on their rackets and their style of game. The Chinese shakehands star (no, not all Chinese are penholders) Liang Ko-liang is a good example of this. He turns up as a variable at every World Championship, spinning or not spinning, attacking or defending.

"There's not a soft chopper like Liang in Sweden," said a discouraged Hans Alser after he and his teammates had just lost the 1971 World Team Championship to the Chinese, who were returning to international competition after a six-year absence brought on by their Cultural Revolution. "Against a hard chop I can get a much better curve on the ball. Well, what can you do? We play the Chinese one hour. We play the others 10,000 hours. Still, if I play normal we win."

Maybe he wins and maybe he doesn't. But one thing's for sure. His opponent Liang is invariably playing with two different kinds of rubber on his racket, the exact surfaces of which are for a time undeterminable. (World-class players, by the way, often use rubber especially made for them that is much better than the kind the average player buys.)

So, O.K., even at the most advanced level of competition, no hard and fast rules about the right playing style or the right kind of rubber to play with can easily (if at all) be made. For example, some say, though others disagree, that the Chinese players usually don't start their extremely fast stroke until the ball hit by the opponent is on their side of the table—this whether they're playing a chopper or a blocker who is more apt than others to get a net, in which case the Chinese player about to hit the ball won't get caught trying to stop his stroke in mid-swing.

Since I'm a blocker and pips-out hitter, when I'm at a World Championships I naturally look for a great player (it doesn't make any difference to me if he uses a penholder or a shakehands grip) who ideally, with my style, I could play like. Or, to put it another equally dreamy way, who plays like me. Only better, of course—much, much better. Such a player I saw at the World Championships in India—a pips-out Chinese named Li Chin-shih.

"The Chinese are the last of the bluebloods of great hitters," said Dick Miles a few years ago. And now, only recently, he's argued that when the pips-out Chinese perfect their kill shots by practicing day after day against the most intense and varied kinds of spin, well, after a while, so perfect is their timing it's as if there isn't any spin on the ball at all and they can just keep hitting in point after point.

An ideal illustration of this thought, which I very much share with Dick, can be seen in the crowd-pleasing Li Chen-shih-Furukawa match I so well remember from Calcutta. Up two games to one in a three-out-of-five-game match but down 10-4 in the fourth to this graceful, ascetic-looking Japanese chopper, Li suddenly, like at a shooting gallery, picked up a gun, fired (bull's-eye!), dropped it, picked up another, fired (bull's-eye!), dropped it—and so on, point after point, until it was 12-all. Then he reloaded and started firing again. Final score: Li 21, Furukawa 14. The Chinese had finished by winning 17 out of the last 21 points.

Of course, all my years in the game or no, I was as impressed as anyone there. It was also very comfortable for me to know that if ever I needed any vindication of my desire to play like a winner with the bat I particularly wanted to, it was there. And so it would always be, in different ways, for many other people as well, whether they played pips-out or pips-in.

For a number of years in this country, where table tennis is just now starting to develop, our top players have wrestled with this question of whether they ought to play with the inverted, flat-surface racket or not.

And as often as not have changed their minds twice over about it.

Dell Sweeris, who was on the 1969 U.S. team to the Munich World's, once switched from inverted to pimple because, he said, the flat-surface racket involved him in a lot more necessary motion, hence his loop was leaving him open to quick deflecting block shots or, if he played a chopper, to getting his own spin back again.

However, after Dell had switched to pips-out, he found that it wasn't so easy to hit against choppers. Turns out he'd been practicing not hitting with that inverted racket but looping, and too often he still wanted to spin a ball that he ought to kill. Also, since now, with the pips-out racket, he didn't have a loop to open the point with—that wasn't so good either. Also he'd have to learn to push and block much more aggressively than he'd been doing.

So what did he do? He switched back to inverted again. He wanted to be the National Champion—which meant he had to beat our two best players of the time, D-J Lee, our perennial U.S. Open Champion, and young John Tannehill, who was to be with our "Ping-Pong diplomacy" team in China.

"When Lee loops to you from out deep," said Dell, "you block the shot back and move in to hit your forehand. If you hit this shot with the pimples, Lee will get too many of them back, will be able to get himself set again. But if you can loop this ball with the inverted, you'll most likely win the point every time."

But then against the best U.S. chopper, Fuarnado Roberts, Dell's own inverted spin really loads up the ball on its return and, at this point in time and space, he can't kill with the flat-surfaced racket as well as he did with the pimples.

It all sounds technically correct, of course. And yet throughout these changes one fact obviously remains constant. That Sweeris, like many another good player, continued to have problems whichever racket he chose and so never did become our National Champion.

As for John Tannehill, who was never our National Champion either, well, he may make more sense to you than Sweeris. When asked for the nth time why he'd switched, at least for the moment, to pimpled sponge, he practically yelled, "Because it's more fun! You understand? More fun! I can feel the ball!"

chapter eight

As you've probably concluded by now, there's no tried-and-true way for anyone both to have fun and be a winner at table tennis. As it happens, I'm one of those players—like our former 4-time U.S. Champion and World Mixed Doubles Champion Erwin Klein—who has never done any circuit training, never the least toe-touching exercise, to get myself in shape to play this sport. The only regimen that I and many players of my generation followed was to play as often as we could and as much as we could (which meant of course hours at a time).

Yet in 17 years of tournament competition I've been extremely fortunate in that I've always been rather physically fit. Not once in 17 years have I ever had to default a match because of sickness or injury. Sure, I've had bad colds, and once I had over a 100-degree temperature and was very weak and shaky from being sick to my stomach the night before, but I played on. One time I had a bad case of bursitis,

keeping physically and mentally fit

but, since my opponent didn't know it, I just managed to keep raising my arm long enough to block ball after ball, while he obliged by looping everything off the table to allow me to win the match.

Another time, nervous over a 2-hour delayed flight from New York to Cleveland and for sure a missed connection to a tournament in Akron, I took a double martini before lunch, later fainted at 30,000 feet, and was taken off the plane on a stretcher into a waiting ambulance that, with sirens going off in my ears, sped me like life and death to a hospital.

There, as I was wheeled into the emergency room, I heard, I saw, one person in white say to another person in white (both of them looking much too casually at me), "He's a heart case." Which naturally scared the hell out of me. Here I was, only 36 years old, and yet maybe I was going to die at any minute, all alone, away from my wife and kids, without giving them any farewell line to remember me by. After they'd taken an electrocardiogram, a doctor came in reading my chart and frowning, and when I asked the stupid rhetorical question, "Pretty bad, huh?" he noncommitally said I'd be staying in the hospital for at least 3 or 4 days more.

Fifteen minutes later, an older doctor came in, picked up my chart, looked at it, shook his head, said the other doctor had misread it, said that when I felt up to it I'd be allowed to go. Except, he advised me, I ought not to fly home but take an easy bus ride back.

There was nothing wrong with my heart. So of course I did what any player with the psychic or physical strength I had for the game would do. I rolled off the doctor's table I thought I might die on, ran to a phone, got the long distance call through to the right people in Akron, pleaded with them not to default my matches, urged them to "play around me," then raced out into the street, hailed a cabbie to drive me as fast as he could the 40 or 50 miles to the Firestone Gymnasium, and, on getting there in record time, hurried out to the tables where I quickly played and won 4 matches in a row.

So much in the old days for my physical fitness.

MODERN-DAY PHYSICAL CONDITIONING

I must confess, though, that the sport today is faster and therefore more physically demanding than it was in the '50s or '60s. Still, contrary to what coach after coach might say, my own advice is for you to forget about the physical conditioning and concentrate on the play. Obviously you must have stamina, you must have fast hands and feet, but if you have soul-strength, if you really want to play and care enough about winning, you'll learn how to speed up your skills through the trial and error of actual play and by watching the best players in this country and abroad.

Where, indisputably, conditioning matters most is at a world-class level of play. If your game ever begins to approximate that, then it'll be apparent to you what you'll have to do.

From many a modern day coach's point of view, though, the beginner, the would-be player, often thinks he's much better suited for the sport than he in fact is. Some coaches I know won't let him near the table unless he's first done 3 months of running and rigorous physical training.

U.S. Team Members running and training before the World Championships in Sarajevo, Yugoslavia, Spring, 1973. (Photos by Mal Anderson)

Iranian star Houshang Bozorgzadeh (left) playing against the veteran Laszlo Foldy of Switzerland in the 1973 World Championships in Sarajevo. (Photo by Mal Anderson)

Coordination

Other coaches, while not conditioned to be so strict, insist that beginners at least go through a series of eye, hand, and foot exercises —bouncing the ball on the racket or "dribbling" the ball on the ground with the racket as they hurry through a makeshift slalom.

Houshang Bozorgzadeh, the Iranian star, once told me about some coaches he'd known who'd urged their win-hungry players to keep throwing peanuts or little pieces of candy up in the air. The idea, of course, was for the player to catch them coming down, in his mouth —for hand and eye coordination. "One Iranian," said Houshang with a twinkle, "was so good—honestly—he was like a dog. He could even catch an apple in his mouth." Here Houshang took a little jump, looked up and growled. "Every American would lose to him," he said as I started to laugh. "*You* try to catch an apple and you'd see—you'd break your nose."

Stamina

Houshang also told me about a bicycle-coaching method he saw in Russia 6 years ago. There was a bicycle wheel for the aspiring player to practice on—and an attached speedometer. You took your racket and put it on the wheel and began to stroke—to rub up and follow through,

170

to rub up and follow through, to rub up and follow through—until your arm could just not go up, not even once more.

There was also a 2-step or a 4-step exercise that one did on a stairway: up with the left foot, then down with the left while up with the right, then up or down left, up or down right, backwards and forwards—I don't think I've even got it straight here I so completely believed Houshang when he said nobody could do it for more than 10 minutes—that their legs just wouldn't move after a while.

You can make it a general rule that, as my sports-minded father used to say (he was an ex-four-letter man, later an osteopath standing on his feet all day working on others' muscles), "The legs are the first to go." That is, experts generally agree that your legs show the condition of the rest of you pretty well.

Most table tennis superathletes train in the summer for the coming season, and only during this time do they run long distances up and down hills, mile after mile, to make sure they're in shape. When the season starts and they're competing in tournaments every weekend, there's no need for them to run long distances. What they need to practice then, though for a relatively short time, say 45 minutes a day, is interval sprint running—to increase their speed.

Agility Exercises

More than anything else, competitors at whatever level need agility exercises that train the muscles they'll most need to win matches. Any good coach ought to urge his players to do lots of shadow practice so that they can simulate the actual strokes they'll be using in a game—including the necessary quick returns back from the follow-throughs to the basic ready positions.

To make a player lighter on his feet in a match, the coach can have him practice left-right, backward-forward, in-out movements, can have him run backwards as well as forwards. Can make these movements tougher by having his pupil play with weighted shoes or with little sandbags tied round his calves.

The player ought also to practice quick-start, quick-stop movements. In the Benson and Hedges Jamaican International last year, our number-one player Danny Seemiller went after an irretrievable ball

171

Les Haslem, former Champion and now National Coach of Jamaica. From the looks of him, his students will surely learn the agility exercises they need to train their muscles. (Photo by Neal Fox)

Japanese Women's Team doing warm-up exercises before a tournament. (Photo by Jacob Forsell)

172

U.S. Team Member George Brathwaite, one of the best-conditioned players in the country. Compare his well-developed right (hitting) arm with his left one.

with his racket extended, then flying, and with such quick-start, quick-stop force, that he ended up pivoting round and sitting yogalike on top of the table. Nobody could move that fast unless his hours of practice had alerted him to the need for such split-second timing.

Since body-twist is so important for power nowadays (sometimes a player's hard-hit ball spins the whole upper half of him around so that his back is almost facing his opponent), a number of waist- and shoulder-turning exercises are a must for many a coach. As are sit-ups for the abdominal muscles. And squat rabbit-jumps, hands on legs, to remind the player how necessary it is to bend his knees and strengthen his thighs.

Skipping and jumping rope are of course good for footwork. And become second nature to a player even while he's playing a match. One of our best U.S. competitors, George Brathwaite, after hitting in a key shot or two, can often be seen jogging round the court, hands raised in fists of triumph.

Use of Weights

Another member of our U.S. Team, the 6-time National Champion

173

1967 World Champion Hasegawa lifts his backhand yet keeps a butterfly-balance. (Photo sequence by Chui Fan Liu)

D-J Lee, used to prepare himself for tournaments even as he was driving to them. He'd have one hand on the steering wheel, another out the window doing dumbbell exercises.

Ten years ago, the great Japanese World Champion Hasegawa trained 5 hours a day, 7 days a week. When, near retirement in his late 20s, he played in our '74 U.S. Open, he complained that his stamina wasn't holding up as it used to. Perhaps the reason was he now trained only 3 hours a day, 5 days a week—did, for example, each workout session, a scant 2,000 strokes with a 40-pound dumbbell.

When Not to Practice

A few years ago one of our top players was so into training with weights that he went out to play a 2-out-of-3-game match wearing his 10-pound Ton-a-matic black belt. And as if that wasn't handicap enough, he proceeded with dedicated interest and sobriety to lose two straight by practicing the third-ball attack, which he missed no fewer than 15 times in a row. Such persistence surely showed strength of spirit but had nothing to do with winning table tennis.

Though there are some warm-up exercises designed to increase the experienced player's hand-eye coordination—a game of double

174

bounce, say, where each player hits the ball first on his own side, then on the other—I don't recommend even to the most dedicated carrying them over into the game. Not if you want to win.

Occasionally a player comes out to the table gyrating so enthusiastically that he unconsciously wants to continue his shadow practice even into the game. Repeatedly he'll hold up his hand during play—meaning he's not ready for the serve—and will take half a dozen phantom swings until the umpire tells him to continue. Playing against such a nervous person is something you've just got to get used to.

Table tennis is a jumpy, excitable game—and often a player will find himself doing things instinctively, without really thinking. One guy at our '74 U.S. Open, who'd been practicing in his jump suit but who'd then left off to become absolutely absorbed in watching the best players in the world, almost forgot about his own match (which in the back of his mind he seemed to remember he had to do something to prepare for) and at the last minute went running out to the table, jump suit jacket flapping. Then, scarcely taking a warm-up, he dropped his jump pants—only to discover that in his hurry he'd forgotten to put on his playing shorts.

Sample Exercise Program

There are a lot of hard-working players in the U.S.—and one of them is a Philadelphia police sergeant named Bill Sharpe, an ex-Olympic hop, step, and jump man. Bill, who is now one of the best Over 40 players in the country, was telling me once about his daily exercises.

"Well," he said, "I begin by running 2 miles each morning —which means maybe getting up at 4:30. Then I do 200 sit-ups. Then 50 leg races—that's bicycle movements, for the lower abdominals. Then 25 push-ups—fast as you can, you know. Then ten 100-yard dashes. Then 100 more sit-ups. And another 25—"

"WAIT A MINUTE!" I said. "When do you go to work?"

"Why," said Bill, "this doesn't take but an hour and a half, two hours. In fact, it's only an inkling into what I did when I was on the Olympic team. Anyway, when I get home at night . . ."

(Something about . . . leg press . . . 300 pounds . . .)

"HEY," he said, "aren't you interested? Don't you want to know

175

about my wheat germ oil, soy beans, tiger's milk. . . . You know I don't smoke or drink.''

"No tea?'' I ventured timidly.

"Tea? No, no tea. I told you, I don't smoke or drink. Got 3 boys though. . . . ''

DIET

Most of the players on the circuit are very careful about what they eat. Most agree with D-J Lee, our last world-ranked player, who knows from experience that regular tournament fare, hot dogs and cellophane sandwiches, make him sick—that he's got to have some fruit, a chocolate bar, honey, water, and almost nothing else, maybe some Chinese tea, until after the matches when he can take his time and eat decently.

One reason the Chinese have been so successful at table tennis the world over is that they bring to the World Championships at Nagoya, or Sarajevo, or (ohhh, easy to get sick at) Calcutta, their own food from China and their own special cooks to prepare it.

You Are What You Eat

"You are what you eat,'' somebody once said. Well, if that's the case, and we want to learn more about the professional table tennis athlete, specifically John Tannehill, former U.S. number two, consider the following conversation I had with him a few years back.

I've walked up just as John has pulled out from his bag (it looks very much like the one I keep cigars, cigarettes, a thermos of coffee, candy—comforts in general in) a vial of pills.

"Vitamin B is water soluble,'' Tannehill is saying—and already I've lost his meaning. "And so is Vitamin C. The more water you drink, the more vitamins leave your body through your urine.''

"Like poison,'' somebody else says.

"Oh, now I see,'' I say. "You're talking about how it's not good to drink too much water—or anything—during even a very hot afternoon's play, not if you want to keep the strength of those vitamins in you.''

"That's right,'' says John. "Coke, Pepsi robs the body of its anti-urine stress agents. When you're under stress—as you always are, playing important matches—you need to retain as many vitamins as you can to help you.''

"But if you're losing water, you've got to replace it. You can't dehy—''

"How are the ridges in your tongue?'' John suddenly says to me.

For a moment I wonder what he's driving at. I've been drinking, like any sane person, not only cokes but, the night before, beers with Pradit and Lee, two martinis.

"A completely smooth tongue is best,'' he says, looking at mine and smiling and shaking his head.

"Here,'' he says abruptly, "take one of these,'' and offers me a little bottle of pills he's just pulled out of his bag. "It's got 50 times the MDR of Vitamin B in it.'' Someone has to explain to me that MDR means Minimum Daily Requirement.

"This bottle has Nature's Plus, Super B-50 capsules. But soon you won't be able to buy these supplemental vitamins. The FDA has outlawed them. Big business doesn't want people to go to health food stores. They'd rather they go to Safeways and end up killing themselves.''

Then John reaches down, brings out a bottle of Schiff Wheat Germ Oil. "Take two tablespoons of this,'' he says, "and after half an hour your body will really feel like jumping. It's been proven. Russian athletes going to the Olympics—if they could lift 100 pounds, they could lift 200 after taking this.''

This didn't seem very logical to me, but I didn't argue. "What's it taste like?'' I ask.

"Terrible,'' says Tannehill. Then he puts a hand down, comes up with a bottle of quick energy Alfalfa (Black) Honey. "The blacker it is, the better it is,'' he says.

A teaspoon of that, I think, and I'd throw up.

"It's straight from the bees,'' says John, "untouched by factories. Take it with orange juice before a match.''

John's hand goes down into his bag again. This time he comes up with a "wonder'' juice. A bottle of Eden Carrot Juice from Germany. "This has lots of Vitamin A, to make you see well,'' he says. "It's also a protein-synthesizing agent. Protein needs a Vitamin A catalyst. A pint of this a day will cure any disease.''

177

Down goes his hand into the bag. Up it comes with Norway Sardines. "Steak, chicken," John is saying, "have so much fat. Besides, the animals might have been drugged."

Mentally, I jump at the sardines. Finally, something good for me I like. "A few of those on some crackers," I say, "and a very cold, very dry martini, and I'd—"

"The worst possible thing is alcohol," says John, interrupting me. "It robs the liver of Vitamin B."

"Here," he says, offering me that little bottle of pills again. "Nature's Plus. Go on, take one. You'll play a lot better."

I think, "What the hell, can one do me any harm?" I take one, swallow it down with some Coke.

Then I say, "Look, I don't play so bad anyway, right? Most of this is just mind over matter. Better you eat what tastes good, what you like."

"It works the other way, too," says John with a smile—as if he's heard this mindless argument before. "There's also matter over mind."

Chui, another of our U.S. team players, has come by. He's stopped to tell Tannehill he's wanted for a match, and has listened for a moment to the conversation. "An almond a day will cure cancer," he says.

"Oh? Why's that?" I ask.

"I don't know," he says with a grin.

MENTAL OR SPIRITUAL STRENGTH

The inseparable complement of keeping physically fit is keeping mentally or spiritually fit. Often the winning source of inspiration, the motivating force, is the image of a loved one. So it was, in part, with the Japanese World Champion Itoh. When his father was sick and Itoh with all his heart wanted to continue his table tennis schooling, his 64-year-old mother worked to make it possible.

Often too it's the face of another great competitor who pushes you towards perfection. So again it was with Itoh. He could never rest, he said, if he knew his rival Kohno was practicing. Could never rest if he knew Kohno was *not* practicing, for then there was always the chance he still had time to surpass him.

The Chinese, particularly, have the motivation to be winners. To begin with, so many people just naturally love the sport. In Canton, I saw, or thought I saw, little boys squatting over mounds of earth hitting an imaginary table tennis ball back and forth over an imaginary net. In Peking I was in a playground where, for team after team, generation after generation, there were all-weather concrete tables with bricks for nets.

Chinese kids grow up to be winners because each one fights primarily not for himself but for the honor of China. In 1971, when the Chinese made a triumphant reentry into the table tennis world, their spirit of nationalism was everywhere apparent. Liang Ko-liang, one of their best players, was one game down and down 17-12 in the second in a 2-out-of-3-game match with the Swedish star Johansson. At which point, a mandarin-suited official, seated on the Chinese bench outside the court behind Johansson and so facing Liang, reached into his breast pocket and pulled out a little red book. Never mind it was only a notebook, it certainly looked like the real thing. Liang saw it held up, Mao-like—a Sacred Heart or a crucifix—and almost mystically pulled the game out.

In 1973, the South Korean women players won the Women's World Team Championship. And since it marked the first time South Korea had won the World Championship in any sport, people wondered how it was done. Through hard work and constant practice, of course, but also with the help of religion. In this case, Buddhism ("Endurance is the most difficult of all disciplines, but it is to the one who endures that the final victory is given"). Recently the Korean coach pointed out how Miss Chung Hyun Sook, one of the world's best women players (she came to this country with her teammates to play in the '75 U.S. Open), followed his advice and served for a time with a Buddhist priest—beginning with his 4 o'clock sermon every morning.

Building Confidence

In *The Will To Win,* Kljuic-Branin's book on the great Yugoslav player Surbek, the interrelation of the body and the spirit may be seen in a simple exercise in which Surbek voluntarily tested his endurance. With his eyes always wide open he would deliberately sit in a darkened room for hours on end watching or not watching the little white table

Surbek, eyes almost as wide as the ball—maybe from that dark room he used to sit in? (Photo by Bora Vojnovic)

tennis ball. Why? So that when later he would be playing important matches it would seem all the bigger, all the clearer to him. So that he could look at the ball, really look at it, and read his opponent's spin better, and could see himself where better to contact the ball, on the top, the bottom, or the side.

No surprise then that, after reading about some of these stars and getting to play them (when finally the USTTA made an effort to bring them to our tournaments here in this country), many of our players were at least somewhat awed by them. Roger Sverdlik, our U.S. Under 17 Champion, played former World Champion Stellan Bengtsson in the '75 U.S. Open and lost the first game by the very unusual score of 21-6. How was it done? Sverdlik seemed so interested, it was as if, even while he was playing this champion, he was watching himself on film—like in that famous Hemingway story where the boy comes back paralyzed from 5 World War I battle campaigns and likes to study maps of where he's been in body but not in mind.

In his second game with Bengtsson, Roger was up 2-0 . . . down 13-2. How was it done? A fellow player watching told Roger that he, Roger, always seemed so amazed, so impressed with Bengtsson's game, that he couldn't play his own. "Good shot! Good shot!" Roger,

180

shaking his head, kept saying. He was nervous of course but, more than that, he was psychically off balance. In one game, he said, he served at least 4 balls into the net because he was trying to keep Bengtsson from spinning. Roger thought he was serving his good serves short—but obviously they weren't short enough. Of course he was hoping Bengtsson would push one ball—so that he could get set. But Roger never could get set.

"I have films of the match," he said later, "but I don't know what happened."

As every winner knows deep down, how good a player you are is all relative—measurable only by the very best in skill and experience. Still, the better you dream you are, the better you really are.

One of the best players on our U.S. Team, Peter Pradit, who before coming to this country had played for Thailand in the prestigious Asian Games and who had trained with some world-class players in Japan, expressed not so long ago the experienced winner's attitude any coach would want for his student. Pradit had just beaten Reisman in a close match (Marty was showing a little endurance of his own by coming out of retirement in his 40s to try to make the U.S. team), and as we began to talk I was amazed that Peter had never heard of the man he'd just beaten.

"You didn't know Reisman had won the English Open, had gotten to the semi's of the World's?"

"No," said Pradit.

"Would it have made any difference if you knew?" I asked him.

"No," said Pradit. "If you're scared, you can't play."

"Can't you ever remember a time when you were scared? When you were young, maybe?"

"No," said Pradit. "I never remember one time."

Whether Pradit was telling the whole truth or not, whether he'd forgotten he'd forgot just that one time he was scared, I could only leave to the mirror of his own self. But I believed him.

Understanding Self

One of our other U.S. team members, Olga Soltesz, who also trained in Japan, told me how Ogimura, the famous Japanese coach, had her doing the expected strenuous exercises. But the advice that most impressed her was his cryptic comment, "You must overcome yourself before you can overcome your opponents."

Perhaps the best way for a coach to teach, for a pupil to learn, is to bring together both body and soul in practice. One way to do this is through some Creative Drama exercises in which every player can learn about self and, by sharing his humanity, about others—players, opponents, who are of course much like self. My Iranian friend, Houshang Bozorgzadeh, using Danny Seemiller and a number of other good players, myself included, demonstrated in an impromptu clinic one day what might be gained from such discipline.

One very interesting exercise involved a Marcel Marceau-like pantomime of one player (Danny) trying to copy another (Houshang). Before they even got to the table to face each other in the alter ego mirror of the playing court, they began practicing—the left-handed Danny trying to do the right-handed Houshang's every inverse move. Of course the idea was to try to understand and anticipate your opponent's or, more deeply, your own actions.

In the beginning, the movements had to be rather predictable—hands out and around clockwise, simulated bird flights, knee bends, bicycle pedaling with the hands, and so on, ad infinitum. One could see in an instant that the exercises were designed to appeal to the imagination—to take the drudgery out of mere mechanical practice.

But when the players got to the table, each taking his turn at being leader, the self-examination began to border on the mystical. It was first eerie, then revelatory, as the players more and more began to synchronize their movements—so that after a while each was beginning to anticipate the other's movements despite their quite different playing styles.

"Some clubs I've been to," said Houshang, looking round at his audience, "put five or six mirrors up, like in a ballet school, and have their players work out privately or in pairs." Like the Chinese, I thought, who, working from films, photos, and notes, trained many of their practice players to be mirror images of the best Japanese, the best Swedes, Yugoslavs, and Hungarians in the world.

Fascinated, we continued our Creative exercises. And as on and on we went, trying to sidestep here, there, swinging a little wildly this

Danny Seemiller, U.S. number 1, as if at prayer. Will he win? Or has he already lost? "There is no real victory or defeat," said Chuang Tse-tung. "There is always both." (Photo courtesy of Houshang Bozorgzadeh)

way and that, trying to keep up with the imaginary little ball hurtling through space we tried to insist was real, not only our dancing master, Mr. Bozorgzadeh, but even the most self-conscious of those who were slowly drawn into the inner circle of this little clinic could grasp the possibilities of the pantomime.

"Table tennis," said Houshang as time ran out and the lesson came to an end, "is the best game to see yourself."

appendix:
laws of table tennis

(Together with Regulations and Recommendations respecting Equipment as adopted for Competition by the United States Table Tennis Association as of March, 1974.)

1. THE TABLE

1.1 The table shall be in surface rectangular, 274 cm. (9 ft.) in length, 152.5 cm. (5 ft.) in width; it shall be supported so that its upper surface, termed the "playing surface," shall lie in a horizontal plane 76 cm. (2 ft. 6 in.) above the floor.

1.2 It shall be made of any material and shall yield a uniform bounce of not less than 22 cm. (8¾ in.) and not more than 25 cm. (9¾ in.) when a standard ball is dropped from a height of 30.5 cm. (12 in.) above its surface.

1.3 The playing surface shall be dark colored, preferably dark green, and matt, with a white line 2 cm. (¾ in.) broad along each edge.

1.4 The lines at the 152.5 cm. (5 ft.) edges, or ends, shall be termed "end lines," and the lines at the 274 cm. (9 ft.) edges, or sides, shall be termed "side lines."

1.5 For doubles, the playing surface shall be divided into halves by a white line 3 mm. (⅛ in.) broad, running parallel to the side lines, termed the "center line." The center line may, for convenience, be permanently marked in full length on the table and this in no way invalidates the table for singles play.

2. THE NET AND ITS SUPPORTS

2.1 The playing surface shall be divided into two "courts" of equal size by a net running parallel to the end lines and 137 mm. (4 ft. 6 in.) from each. The net, with its suspension shall be 183 cm. (6 ft.) in length; along its whole length its upper part shall be 15.25 cm. (6 in.) above the playing surface and its lower part shall be close to the playing surface. It shall be suspended by a cord attached at each end to an upright post 15.25 cm. (6 in.) high; the outside limits of each post shall be 15.25 cm. (6 in.) outside the side line.

3. THE BALL

3.1 The ball shall be spherical, with a diameter of not less than 37.2 mm. (1.46 in.) and not more than 38.2 mm. (1.50 in.). It shall be made of celluloid or a similar plastic, white or yellow and matt; it shall be not less than 2.40 gr. (37 grains) and not more than 2.53 gr. (39 grains) in weight. The standard bounce required shall be not less than 235 mm. (9¼ in.) or more than 255 mm. (10 in.) when dropped from a height of 305 mm. (12 in.) on a specially designed steel block. These heights are measured from the bottom of the ball.

4. THE RACKET

4.1   The racket may be of any size, shape or weight. Its surface shall be dark colored and matt. The blade shall be of wood, continuous, of even thickness, flat and rigid. If the blade is covered on either side, this covering may be either:

4.1.1   Plain ordinary pimpled rubber, with pimples outward, of a total thickness of not more than 2 mm.; or:

4.1.2   "Sandwich," consisting of a layer of cellular rubber surfaced by plain ordinary pimpled rubber turned inwards or outwards, of a total thickness covering either side of not more than 4 mm.

4.2   When rubber is used on both sides of a racket, the colors on the two sides shall be similar; when wood is used for the striking surface on either side it should be dark, either naturally or by being stained, but not painted, in such a way as not to change the friction character of the surface. Each side of the blade, whether used for striking the ball or not, must be of a uniform dark color.

4.3   The part of the blade nearest the handle and gripped by the fingers may be covered with any material for convenience of grip, and is to be regarded as part of the handle. Similarly, if the reverse side of the racket is never used for striking the ball it may be covered with any material as the limitation of covering materials applies only to the striking surface; a stroke with a side covered with any material other than those specified above would, however, be illegal and incur the loss of a point.

5. DEFINITIONS & INTERPRETATIONS

5.1   The player who first strikes the ball during a rally will be termed the server.

5.2   The player who next strikes the ball during a rally will be termed the receiver.

5.3   The period during which the ball is in play will be termed a rally.

5.4   A rally the result of which is not scored will be termed a let.

5.5   A rally the result of which is scored will be termed a point.

5.6   The "racket hand" is the hand carrying the racket, and the "free hand" is the hand not carrying the racket.

5.7   "Struck" means "hit with the racket, carried in the racket hand, or with the racket hand below the wrist." A stroke made with the hand alone, after dropping the racket, or by the racket after it has slipped or been thrown from the hand, is "not good."

5.8   If the ball in play comes in contact with the racket or the racket hand below the wrist, not yet having touched the playing surface on one side of the net since last being struck on the other side, it shall be said to have been "volleyed."

5.9   The "playing surface" shall be regarded as including the top edges of the table, and a ball in play which strikes these latter is, therefore "good" and still in play; if it strikes the side of the table-top below the edge it becomes out of play and counts against the last striker.

5.10 "Around the net" means under or around the projection of the net and its supports outside the table, but not between the end of the net and the post.

5.11 If a player, in attempting to serve, misses the ball altogether he loses a point, because the ball is in play from the moment it is deliberately projected from the hand.

5.12 The part of the playing surface nearest the server and to his right of the center line shall be called the server's right hand court, and to his left the server's left hand court. The part of the playing surface on the other side of the net from the server and to his left of the center line shall be called the receiver's right hand court, and on the server's right the receiver's left hand court.

6. THE ORDER OF PLAY

6.1 In singles, the server shall first make a good service, the receiver shall then make a good return and thereafter server and receiver shall each alternately make a good return.

6.2 In doubles, the server shall first make a good service, the receiver shall then make a good return, the partner of the server shall then make a good return, the partner of the receiver shall then make a good return and thereafter each player alternately in that sequence shall make a good return.

7. A GOOD SERVICE

7.1 The ball shall be placed on the palm of the free hand, which must be stationary, open and flat, with the fingers together and the thumb free. The free hand, while in contact with the ball in service shall at all times be above the level of the playing surface.

7.2 The server must serve so the umpire can see his serve. If the server is serving so the umpire's view is obstructed, the umpire shall warn the server and, on any subsequent serve where his view is obstructed and he has any doubt about the correctness of the serve, the umpire will call a fault.

Service shall then begin by the server projecting the ball by hand only, without imparting spin, near vertically upwards (a 45 degree allowance from vertical all around), so that the ball be visible at all times to the umpire and so that it visibly leaves the palm.

As the ball is then descending from the height of its trajectory it shall be struck so that it touches first the server's court and then, passing directly over or around the net, the receiver's court.

In doubles, the ball shall touch first the server's right half-court or the center line on his side of the net, pass over or around the net, then touch the receiver's right half-court or the center line on his side of the net.

At the moment of the impact of the racket on the ball in service, the ball shall be behind the end line of the server's court or an imaginary extension thereof.

Strict observance of the prescribed method of service may be waived where the umpire is notified, before play begins, that compliance is prevented by physical disability.

8. A GOOD RETURN

8.1   The ball, having been served or returned in play, shall be struck so that it passes directly over or around the net and touches directly the opponent's court. If the ball, having been served or returned in play, returns with its own impetus over or around the net, it may be struck while still in play so that it touches directly the opponent's court. If the ball, in passing over or around the net, touches it or its supports it shall be considered to have passed directly.

9. IN PLAY

9.1   The ball is in play from the moment at which it is projected from the hand in service until:

9.2   It has touched one court twice consecutively.

9.3   It has, except in service, touched each court alternately without having been struck with the racket intermediately.

9.4   It has been struck by a player more than once consecutively.

9.5   It has touched a player or anything he wears or carries, except his racket or his racket hand below the wrist.

9.6   It has been volleyed.

9.7   It has touched any object other than the net, supports, or those referred to above.

9.8   It has, in a doubles service, touched the left half-court of the server or of the receiver.

9.9   It has, in doubles, been struck by a player out of proper sequence, except as provided in law 16.

9.10   It has, under the Expedite System, been returned by thirteen successive good returns of the receiving player or pair.

10. A LET

10.1   The rally is a let:

10.2   If the ball served, in passing over or around the net, touch it or its supports, provided the service be otherwise good or be volleyed by the receiver.

10.3   If a service be delivered when the receiver or his partner is not ready, provided always that a player may not be deemed to be unready if he or his partner attempt to strike at the ball.

10.4   If, owing to an accident not within his control, a player fail to make a good service or return.

10.5   If it be interrupted for correction of a mistake in playing order or ends.

10.6   If it be interrupted for application of the Expedite System.

10.7   Ball fractured in play: If the ball splits or becomes otherwise fractured in play, affecting a player's return, the rally is a let. It is the umpire's duty to stop play, recording a let, when he has reason to believe that the ball is fractured or imperfect;

and to decide those cases in which the faulty ball is clearly fractured in actually going out of play, and in no way has handicapped the player's return, so that the point should be scored. In all cases of doubt, however, he should declare a let.

10.8 Fixtures: A moving spectator, a neighboring player, a sudden noise, i.e. any neighboring object in movement (except a partner) should be regarded as an accident not under control, interference from which implies a let. A stationary spectator, fixed seating, the umpire, the light, a nearby table, a continuous sound of even volume, i.e. any relatively constant or motionless hazard, should not be so regarded, and complaint against interference from it during play should be regarded as void.

10.9 If it be interrupted by the intrusion of another ball in the playing area. Even if this ball does not distract the players, the course of the game may bring it to the attention of one of the players, breaking his concentration. The let should be called immediately when another ball intrudes in the playing area.

11. A POINT

11.1 Except as provided in law 10, a player shall lose a point:

11.2 If he fails to make a good service.

11.3 If, a good service or a good return having been made by his opponent, he fail to make a good return.

11.4 If he, or his racket or anything that he wears or carries, touch the net or its supports while the ball is in play.

11.5 If he, or his racket or anything that he wears or carries, move the playing surface while the ball is in play.

11.6 If his free hand touch the playing surface while the ball is in play.

11.7 If, before the ball in play shall have passed over the end lines or side lines without having touched the playing surface on his side of the net since being struck by his opponent, it comes in contact with him or anything he wears or carries.

11.8 If he volleys the ball, except as provided in Law 10.2.

11.9 If, in doubles, he strikes the ball out of proper sequence, except as provided in Law 16.

11.10 If, under the Expedite System, his service and the twelve following strokes of the serving player or pair be returned by good returns of the receiving player or pair.

12. A GAME

12.1 A game shall be won by the player or pair first scoring 21 points, unless both players or pairs shall have scored 20 points, when the winner of the game shall be the player or pair first scoring 2 points more than the opposing player or pair.

13. A MATCH

13.1 A match shall consist of one game or the best of three or best of five games.

13.2 Play shall be continuous throughout, except that either player or pair is entitled to claim a rest period of not more than five minutes duration between the third and fourth game of a match.

13.3   Note: This law defines a contest between two players or pairs. A contest consisting of a group of individual matches between two sides is usually distinguished as a "team match" or "tie."

14. THE CHOICE OF ENDS AND SERVICE

14.1   The choice of ends and the right to serve or receive first in a match shall be decided by the toss of a coin. The winner of the toss may choose the right to serve or receive first and the loser shall then have the choice of ends or vice versa; the winner of the toss may, if he prefers it, require the loser to make first choice.

14.2   In doubles, the pair who have the right to serve the first five services in any game shall decide which partner shall do so. In the first game of a match the opposing pair shall then decide similarly which shall be the first receiver. In subsequent games the serving pair shall choose their first server and the first receiver will then be established automatically to correspond with the first server as provided in law 15.

15. THE CHANGE OF ENDS AND SERVICE

15.1   The player or pair who started at one end in a game shall start at the other in the immediately subsequent game and so on, until the end of the match. In the last possible game of the match the players or pairs shall change ends when first either player or pair reaches the score 10.

15.2   In singles, after five points, the receiver shall become the server and the server the receiver, and so on until the end of the game or the score 20-20, or until the introduction of the Expedite System.

15.3   In doubles, the first five services shall be delivered by the selected partner of the pair who have the right to do so and shall be received by the appropriate partner of the opposing pair. The second five services shall be delivered by the receiver of the first five services and received by the partner of the first server. The third five services shall be delivered by the partner of the first server and received by the partner of the first receiver. The fourth five services shall be delivered by the partner of the first receiver and received by the first server. The fifth five services shall be delivered as the first five and so on in sequence until the end of the game or the score 20-20, or until the introduction of the Expedite System.

15.4   From the score 20-20, or if the game is being played under the Expedite System, the sequence of serving and receiving shall be the same but each player shall deliver only one service in turn until the end of the game.

15.5   The player or pair who served first in a game shall receive first in the immediately subsequent game, and so on until the end of the match.

15.6   In each game of a doubles match the initial order of receiving shall be opposite to that in the preceding game. In the last possible game of a doubles match, the receiving pair shall alter its order of receiving when first either pair reaches the score 10.

16. OUT OF ORDER OF ENDS OR SERVICE

16.1 If the players have not changed ends when ends should have been changed, they shall change ends as soon as the mistake is discovered, unless a game has been completed since the error, when the error shall be ignored. In any circumstances, all points scored before the discovery shall be reckoned.

16.2 If by mistake a player serves or receives out of his turn, play shall be interrupted as soon as the mistake is discovered and shall continue with that player serving or receiving who, according to the sequence established at the beginning of the match, should be server or receiver respectively at the score that has been reached. In any circumstances, all points scored before discovery shall be reckoned.

17. EXPEDITE SYSTEM

17.1 If a game be unfinished fifteen minutes after it has begun, the rest of that game and the remaining games of the match shall proceed under the Expedite System. Thereafter, each player shall serve one service in turn and, if the service and twelve following strokes of the serving player or pair be returned by good returns of the receiving player or pair, the server shall lose the point. If time was called during a rally, the player who served that rally shall serve first. If time was called between rallies, the receiver of the last serve shall serve next.

18. CLOTHING

18.1 Players will not wear white or light colored clothing (solid) which might tend to distract or unsight the opponent. Any badge or lettering on a playing garment must not be so large or conspicuous as to break disturbingly its uniform dark color. The decision as to the offense under this law will be with the referee.

index

191